*James O'Halloran SDB*

# LIVING CELLS

For all the youth whom I had the privilege of serving down the years, more especially for those in the *barrios* of La Colmena and La Ferroviaria, Quito, Ecuador, from whom I learned so much.

James O'Halloran SDB

# LIVING CELLS

## DEVELOPING
## SMALL CHRISTIAN COMMUNITY

Revised Edition

**DOMINICAN PUBLICATIONS**
**ORBIS BOOKS**

First published 1984 by
Dominican Publications
St Saviour's, Dublin 1, Ireland

Published in USA and Canada by
Orbis Books
Maryknoll, New York 10545

ISBN 0-907271-32-4 (Dominican Publications)
ISBN 0-88344-288-4 (Orbis Books)

© James O'Halloran

---

**Library of Congress Cataloging in Publication Data**

O'Halloran, James.
  Living Cells

  Bibliography: p.
  1. Christian Communities — Catholic Church. 2. Catholic
Church — Developing countries. I. Title.
BX2347.7.038 1984     250       83-22076
ISBN 0-88344-288-4 (pbk)

---

Design by Edward McManus

Typeset and printed by
The Leinster Leader Ltd
Naas, Co. Kildare, Ireland

The Scripture quotations in this volume are from the Revised
Standard Version of the Bible (Catholic Edition) copyrighted
1966 by the Division of Christian Education of the National
Council of Churches of Christ in the USA

# CONTENTS

The company of those who believed were of one heart and soul, and no one said that any of the things which he possessed was his own, but they had everything in common. And with great power the apostles gave their testimony to the resurrection of the Lord Jesus, and great grace was upon them all. There was not a needy person among them, for as many as were possessors of lands or houses sold them, and brought the proceeds of what was sold and laid it at the apostles' feet; and distribution was made to each one as any had need.

Acts 4:32-37

## ACKNOWLEDGMENTS

First of all I must thank the people, especially the youth, of La Colmena and La Ferroviaria, Quito, Ecuador. It was in those *barrios* (a *barrio* is a district, usually a poor one) that I had the basic experience which made this work possible.

There are groups to thank in Dublin (Gardiner Street, Mount Merrion, Crumlin, and Sean McDermott Street). In sharing with them I have been enormously enriched.

I am deeply grateful also to all those people and groups, too numerous to mention, in Africa, the Americas, and elsewhere who shared their experience of the small Christian community with me. Fr José Marins, Sister Teolide Trevisan, and Father Balty Janacek (San Antonio, Texas) were particularly helpful. For more than a decade Father José and Sister Teolide have been tirelessly promoting small Christian communities up and down the Americas and elsewhere in the world.

I should like to thank the various people in Africa who kindly teamed up with me in giving workshops on the subject of small Christian community: Fr Jack McHugh and Joan in Sierra Leone (Jack deeply enriched my theological understanding of the small Christian community); Mike and Tony in Liberia; Máiréad, Edel, and John in Ghana; Florence, Tony, Lar, and Thecla in Zimbabwe; Tony, Lorenzo, Joe, Brian, Noel, Mr Mulenga, and Mr Chita in Zambia; and Paul, Francis, Margaret, and Max in Kenya. From all of these I learned much.

A word of gratitude also to the pastors who invited me to their dioceses to share experiences:

Cardinal Otunga (Nairobi, Kenya), Bishops Potani (Solwezi, Zambia), de Jong (Ndola, Zambia), Lamont and Muchabaiwa (Mutare, Zimbabwe), Dalieh (Cape Palmas, Liberia), Owusu (Sunyani, Ghana), Azzolini (Makene, Sierra Leone), Archbishop Ganda (Freetown, Sierra Leone), and Fr John O'Riordan C.S.Sp. (Apostolic Administrator of Kenema, Sierra Leone). Thanks to Father Tony Byrne C.S.Sp., whose idea the African project was in the first place, and to MISEREOR (Germany) for partially funding the venture in cooperation with the local churches.

Before leaving prelates, I must express my gratitude to Bishop Leonidas Proaño, Riobamba, Ecuador. On more than one occasion he was extremely helpful to me. And thanks to Evangelical Methodist Bishop Mortimer Arias from Bolivia for useful suggestions regarding this book.

Action from Ireland (AFRI) gave me great encouragement in the work to promote small Christian communities and financial assistance so that I could study them at first hand in Brazil and elsewhere in the Americas. I am grateful to the organisation.

I thank my Salesian confreres very sincerely for backing my apostolate to the communities, particularly our Provincial, Fr Joseph Harrington SDB, and our ex-Provincial, Father Michael Hicks SDB. And I thank those confreres directly involved with this publication: Father Patrick McQuaid SDB, Dominic McEvoy SDB, and Francis Dowling SDB.

Finally, I should like to thank my joint publishers, Dominican Publications, Dublin, and Orbis Books, New York for having been unfailingly helpful. A word of gratitude also to a helpful typist, Maria, and to Mike Burke.

## INTRODUCTION

This book is the fruit particularly of the past twelve years during which I have had the good fortune to work and share with small Christian communities in Latin America mainly, but substantially also in Africa, Ireland, and elsewhere.

It is born of experience, and it speaks to experience. I hope that, as the reader's practical knowledge of the small Christian community grows, she/he will find it increasingly meaningful.

The first edition would seem to have been of special help to lay animators and to ordinary lay members of communities. This expanded and revised edition was written with largely the same people in mind. But I would also hope that priests and religious might find it of assistance as a pastoral companion.

The first edition grew out of a largely Catholic experience. The same is true of the present volume. Nevertheless, judging from the feedback, that first attempt seems to have been helpful to persons of other Christian denominations as well.

Specifically, I am treating of small Christian communities. Much of what is said regarding these communities, however, is valid for all groups — not least for those of youth. There is indeed a vital connection between the youth group and the small Christian community.

There is a point which I should like to emphasise. *This is not a handbook* for the small Christian community. The essentials of small Christian communities are to be found in groups irrespective of where they are in the world. For the rest, they adapt very much to local circumstances. Like the

Gospel they must be integrated into the culture where they are being introduced. So please treat this book as a point of reference and not as a blueprint.

In the first edition I used the description *basic Christian community*. You will find in the present work that I have abandoned this description in favour of *small Christian community,* which is the term used in Africa.

The reason why I have done so is that the designation *basic Christian community* was conflicting with the vision of Church that was growing in my mind and, I believe, in reality too. I was increasingly visualising the Church as a series of open concentric circles; as ever-widening communities with small Christian community at the core and not as something in layers with small Christian community at the bottom.

Of course the term *basic community* is meant to convey that the community is composed of poor people. Very often, when I asked groups what they thought basic Christian community meant, however, they felt that it suggested something at the bottom of a hierarchical pile.

Small Christian communities either have all the characteristics of the universal Church or are on the way to acquiring them. It would therefore be more accurate to describe them as small *ecclesial* communities (integral cells of the Church); at least when with time they have acquired all the features of the Church. In Latin America, for example, the groups are commonly referred to as *basic ecclesial communities*. In the English-speaking world, however, they are popularly called *basic Christian communities* or *small Christian communities*. This is another reason why I adopt the latter term. In the end, it is the reality more than the name which counts.

During workshops on small community a frequent question relates to how the group fits into the Church at large. The small Christian community is new wine and requires a new wineskin. The new wineskin is the revitalised Church emerging in the wake of Vatican II. I try to provide an answer in Chapter Five and Section V.

Nearly always you find that a single gender pronoun, usually the masculine form, is used throughout a book, where the appropriate gender is not obvious. In the course of this book I have tried to use terms which cover both genders. But there are times when this causes the most complicated grammatical tangles. In those situations I settled for varying the gender from one part of the book to another.

## PART I

## THE ORIGIN AND GROWTH OF THE SMALL CHRISTIAN COMMUNITY

# 1

## THE ORIGIN AND GROWTH
## OF THE SMALL CHRISTIAN COMMUNITY

I was accepting a series of questions with which to orientate a course on the small Christian community.

"Who was the founder?" asked one student.

The question could be answered on the spot: Jesus Christ.

The history of the small Christian community is, in fact, as old as the Church and as recent as the supermarket. Insofar as its origins go back to the New Testament, it is as old as Jesus Christ. Insofar as it is the core group of a Church where *communion* and *mission* are emphasised, it has a fresh appearance.

*Point of Origin*

It might be difficult to pinpoint where precisely in the world core community first arose in modern times. The Spirit, after all, breathes where he will. It was, however, in Latin America that it made most headway: in the late fifties and early sixties, groups of this nature surfaced in Brazil, Chile, Honduras, and Panama. They then spread to the whole sub-continent.

There were key moments in the history of the communities: those moments in which they were approved and launched by the bishops:

(a) at the Conference of Latin American Bishops held in Medellin, Columbia, 1968:

(b) at the Synod of Bishops, Rome, 1974, owing to the intervention of the then Archbishop Pironio from Argentina;

(c) in *Evangelii nuntiandi* (58) of Paul VI, 1975;*

(d) AMECEA (Association of Member Episcopal Conferences in Eastern Africa) made the establishment of small Christian communities a priority at their Nairobi meeting, 1976;

(e) at Puebla, in 1979, the Latin American bishops wholeheartedly endorsed core communities and re-echoed the sentiments of Paul VI by seeing in them "a sign of hope for the Church";

(f) and, finally, Pope John Paul II in his message to the Brazilian groups, 1980, said: "Above all, it makes me very happy to renew now the confidence which my memorable predecessor, Pope Paul VI, manifested in the small Christian communities."[1]

Among other things, John Paul went on to stress that the small Christian community is *ecclesial:* we are not talking, therefore, of a group which

---

*The Holy Father says that the small Christian communities offer hope for the whole Church provided that they are faithful to its teaching, united to the local and universal Church, and avoid thinking themselves superior to other groups and movements. He also urges them to avoid hiving themselves off from the mainstream of the faithful and encourages them to grow in missionary consciousness, fervour, dedication and zeal.

merely enriches the Church with some special charism, such as a concern for the poor, or a zeal for spreading wholesome Christian literature; rather are we talking of a group that is itself truly a *cell* of the Church. He insisted also on the need for lay-animators to be *in communion with their pastors, prepared in the faith,* and *of exemplary life.*

## Living Cells

In an interview at Crumlin, Dublin, a few years ago, Cardinal Silva Henriquez of Santiago, Chile, gave a good thumbnail sketch of what small Christian community is, and showed besides how much the Latin American bishops pin their hopes upon it:

The small Christian community has served us wonderfully well in Latin America. That sub-continent created and continues to support and direct such groups. The small community is a living cell within the Church; a small-scale group with human warmth; a group in which the Gospel can be lived totally; a nucleus that projects itself into the wider community, be it parish or diocese. A cell such as this will be an effective instrument of evangelization and will transform world structures that are nowadays so materialistic. This is a noble ideal; an ideal which the Latin American bishops hope to achieve through the small communities. Perhaps there is something in this for Ireland.[2]

## Factors favouring Emergence

There were various factors which favoured the

emergence of lay-oriented small Christian communities in Latin America.

Not least of these was a shortage and maldistribution of priests.

A growing individualism also made it imperative that efforts be made at relating persons to one another.

Then the simple faith of ordinary people contributed to an environment where innovation and creativity were possible.

And there was the example and challenge of the Protestant denominations. They were more conversant with the Bible than Catholics, and their religious gatherings had more vitality and participation than the Catholic liturgy.

There was also a longing that the Church should muster its forces and develop the instruments to tackle the injustices that were enslaving the overwhelming majority of the people.

Most telling of all was the effect of persecution which emboldened Christians, who overcame the initial fright of seeing their leaders suffer and die, to answer the call of their bishops and regroup in small communities.


*Not All Smooth*

It was not as if everything went smoothly with the small Christian community in Latin America. In some places groups sprang up readily and spread quickly, yet they disappeared as rapidly as they came. The reason? *There was no true conversion:* no renewal of persons, community, or organisation.

We could perhaps analyse more closely why

some communities failed and thus we can learn from their mistakes.

There were those groups which faded because they were manipulated by some political movement. Socially aware and active they indeed became, but they forgot about the Gospel.

The other side of that particular coin took the form of exclusively spiritual groups which revelled in their pious exercises while ignoring the needy.

Sometimes the Scriptures were used in an unenlightened fashion. Parts were taken out of context or interpreted literally. And the groups became sectarian and sterile. Why make a pother about setting the earth to rights if the end is nigh?

Still others failed because they were continually in conflict with their pastors, with the Church that they labelled *institutional*. They would listen to no one save themselves and played the role of prophets while cutting themselves off from the successors of the apostles.

Now constructive criticism of our Church is a duty. When Jewish dietary laws obstructed unity in the early Church, Paul thrashed matters out with Peter in no uncertain fashion. Notwithstanding this altercation Paul loved Peter and was loyal to him. Criticism made in loyalty can be constructive. It is the reckless kind that has to be avoided.

Sometimes the small Christian community was invaded by the mentality of the consumer society. Where there was efficiency, it was felt results must automatically follow. No room was made for the cross or for what humanly looked like blundering. In the Christian existence there is neither resurrection nor salvation without the cross, without death. The cross and resurrection are interwoven in the fabric of our entire lives, which reflect the tension of

Christ's own life: a life in which he stood trans-figured on Tabor and sweated blood in Gethsemane. "Truly, truly, I say to you, unless a grain of wheat falls into the earth and dies, it remains alone; but if it dies, it bears much fruit" (John 12:24).

Finally, having pointed out where some communities have gone wrong, let me stress that the overwhelming majority of them have had no such difficulties. We must be careful not to distort the picture.

## The United States of America

Groups have begun in Illinois, Florida, Texas, New Mexico, and California, mostly among people of Latin American origins. These people are engaged in a struggle for human and civil rights within the United States system. Despite this, or perhaps because of it, they also have a great sensitivity towards the sufferings of their brothers and sisters in the Third World and see it as a mission to awaken their adopted land on the issue.

The communities in the United States look to Latin America for inspiration. With time they must discover their own identity.

## Africa

There has been significant progress in Africa.

In *East Africa* the AMECEA bishops, as already noted, made the establishment of small Christian communities a priority in 1976. Groups are spreading throughout the region.

In *Southern Africa* too we find the communities in Swaziland, for instance, and in Mozambique since independence. Zimbabwe also has shown interest in the groups and tentative efforts are being made to organise them in the diocese of Mutare, formerly Umtali.

*West Africa* has seen the beginnings of the small Christian community. Sierra Leone, for example, has shown considerable interest, and core groups are forming. Liberia (Cape Palmas) and Ghana (Sunyani) are now on the move.

The Pastoral Centre at Kenema, Sierra Leone, has done much to promote the communities. It has provided courses for people from Sierra Leone itself, from other West African countries, and indeed from the whole continent and beyond.

In 1982 an intensive and possibly unique experience of learning about, and *living,* small Christian community was organised at the centre. There were thirty-nine participants, which was too many. Thirty would have been quite sufficient. And what a diverse group it was. Twenty-eight were from Africa and the remaining eleven from America, Europe, Australia, and Asia. The countries of origin represented within the group were: Sierra Leone, the Gambia, Liberia, Ghana, Nigeria, Zambia, Zimbabwe, Ireland, Holland, Australia, the United States, New Zealand, Australia, and Papua-New Guinea. There were nuns, priests, a brother, a laywoman, and many laymen. There was a hospital matron, a sister tutor, a post-office sorter, members of the pastoral institute staff, and a fair representation of parish clergy, teachers, and catechists. I myself was among the resource persons.

I felt that, if such a diverse group could together form a small Christian community, it would be a minor miracle. To the eternal credit of the group let it be said that they formed an impressive community, despite the inevitable tensions arising from such diversity, and they returned to their places of origin determined to put what they had learned into practice.

In evaluating the four-month course, the participants agreed that the objective of learning about small Christian community through a living experience as well as through intellectual input had been achieved. The course had in fact exceeded their expectations.

It was a notable achievement also for a young Church in a developing country, despite problems of communication, energy and water supplies, to run a course of this kind successfully. This was noted by Archbishop Ganda of Freetown and Bo who said:

> It is indeed a healthy sign of progress for the young Churches of Africa that we no longer depend solely on centres overseas in order to hold a course at this level. It is a sign of a coming of age and the taking of responsibility for our own development.[3]

What the archbishop says is true, but it is also true that the participants in the course, many from more established Churches, through their witness and fieldwork contributed greatly to the young local Church.

Kenema is planning similar experiences for the future, and could become the formative influence for West Africa that the pastoral institute at Gaba (Kenya) is for East Africa and the pastoral centre at Lumko (Transkei) is for Southern Africa.

In certain parts of West Africa, such as Sierra Leone, Christians are a tiny minority among

Muslims and Animists. So the fostering of Christian groups is not just a matter of convenience, but a condition for survival. This is not to imply that comunities should turn in upon themselves. Quite the contrary. But it is only when Christians rally into small groups which are outgoing that they integrate effectively with their predominantly Muslim surroundings. This gives an experience like that of Kenema a further relevance.

*Problems*

There are certain difficulties that frequently preoccupy African groups:
—lack of leaders and, therefore, of continuity; or the presence of leaders who are too domineering and unwilling to relinquish their position
—lack of commitment
—overdependence on the priest
—divisions caused by tribalism, culture, language, and religion
—tyrannical fears arising from the culture (superstition, witchcraft . . .)
—the failure to relate religion to life and its problems
—an unconcern regarding social justice
—the setting aside of youth and women.

The African communities are now developing a strong awareness of questions of social justice. This can be seen from the statement issued by the Symposium of Bishops Conferences of Africa and Madagascar after their sixth General Assembly held at Yaounde, Cameroons, on July 1981.[4]

## French-speaking Africa

Thus far I have been dealing with the areas of Africa where English is the common language, for those are the parts that I know best. French-speaking Africa (e.g. Zaire, Upper Volta) is not lagging behind. There are numerous groups, deeply involved with the realities of life.

## Asia

From Asia one hears of small Christian communities operating in the *Philippines, Indonesia, and Pakistan.*

The Philippines is a largely Catholic country. In its socio-political environment, as in Latin America, the problem is one of gradually raising people's awareness of social injustice, so that they may struggle to overcome it.

There are interesting stirrings in Pakistan, which shares the West African problem as to how best establish the groups in an overwhelmingly Muslim society. Fr L. Mascarenhas, who works there, has the following to say:

> I do think we, as a Church, need more of these small intensive groups living in Muslim surroundings, open to the Spirit speaking to them through their neighbours, and allowing things to happen. In such a setting, despite the adverse press and news media, we shall have beautiful stories to tell the Church at large. We can become a leaven of the Good News in the world today.[5]

Father Mascarenhas relates how, through simple sharing, his little community won acceptance from their Muslim neighbours in a block of flats.

Whether it be East or West Europe, small Christian communities are to be found. In the East we encounter them in Russia (among the Orthodox), in Hungary, and in Poland.

In the West they exist in France (where they are most mature) in Italy, Belgium, Switzerland, and in the Federal German Republic. There are also rustlings in England and Ireland.

Europe has rich and deep religious and secular traditions; so it is much more difficult for a fresh initiative to gain acceptance there than in the Third World.

In Western Europe groups have existed often tenuously on the shadowy margins of the Church; while in Eastern Europe they have not been greatly encouraged by the Church and not at all encouraged by the state.

But times are changing. In the West bishops are increasingly putting their hopes in the small communities. And committed Christians are for their part seeing that separating themselves from the mainstream of the Church is not the answer. Rather must they strive, without giving up their prophetic character, to realise their quite legitimate demand for communion and participation within its confines.

In the East too there are tentative pointers towards accommodation, such as the acceptance of student groups with their chaplains in Poland and the October 1977 communique of the Hungarian bishops which allows small Christian communities to function provided they have a priest animator.

There are salient factors which account for the growth of core groups around the globe.

In Latin America the desire to remedy social injustice brings folk together. These inequities are seen as enslaving people for whose freedom Christ died. The thinking victims of oppression simply cannot believe that wretched, painful lives and premature death is the design of the good God for them. And they are right.

African culture has always had a strong sense of community, even before missionaries arrived. Whereas in the industrialised countries we might tend to say, "I am because I am", an African would be more inclined to declare, "I am because we are". It would be most difficult for an African to conceive of an identity in isolation from the community.

In the more affluent countries the awful isolation and alienation among people caused by materialism create a longing for togetherness.

There is nothing wrong with fostering a sense of togetherness. The question is togetherness for what. For *service* surely. I believe that social justice should be as burning an issue in the affluent countries as in the poor ones. The reason is that, if the First World were to look for the roots of its wealth, it would find them deep in the misery of the Third. Poor nations are poor largely because rich nations exploit them. And then, of course, even in the wealthy countries there are twilight zones of deprivation that need seeing to.

The small Christian community is a growing phenomenon. As such it is hard to quantify. Those engaged in this apostolate have been far too busy to stop and work on worldwide statistics. They calculate that in Brazil there are 80,000 small Christian communities and approximately 150,000 in all of Latin America.

By 1983 there were 10,000 communities in East Africa.

There comes a time in spring when we look out upon a field that has been planted with grain and, although the brown earth predominates, we can see the all-pervading green suggestion of tender wheat blades. It is even so with the communities. When we look on the Church in the world today, although the institution predominates, there is everywhere the green suggestion of small Christian communities.

# PART II

---

## WHAT IS SMALL CHRISTIAN COMMUNITY?

# 2

## WHAT IS SMALL CHRISTIAN COMMUNITY?

The historic Latin American bishops' meeting at Medellin, Columbia, 1968, which put the Church in that sub-continent firmly on the side of the poor and oppressed, very aptly described the small Christian community as the *Church in nucleus*.

The term *nucleus* implies two things: we are talking of entities that are *small-scale* and at the *centre* of more enlarged Christian and human groupings. For me, it presupposes a *community*

SMALL CHRISTIAN COMMUNITY
PARISH / AREA COMMUNITY
DIOCESAN COMMUNITY
UNIVERSAL CHURCH COMMUNITY
WORLD COMMUNITY

*vision* of the Church, a series of communities rippling out in ever-widening concentric circles from the small Christian community, the most localised unit at the centre. And these various communities are not separate from the world but are immersed in the world at every phase, as shown in diagram (p. 25).

A community vision of the Church would also mean that the members share their lives. This they do spiritually (by worshipping together), emotionally (through friendship), intellectually (by sharing ideas), and materially (by being generous with earthly goods).

I have purposely left all the above circles open, because a Christian community of its very nature must be open to all other communities: either it inter-relates and interacts with them or it ceases to be Christian.

I recall having a long, good-humoured dialogue with a community in Kenya which tended to be closed and clannish. They kept on talking about having to have *laws*. By this they seemed to mean *rules* that would turn them into something of an exclusive club.

I argued that Christ only gave us one law, that we love one another as he loves us; and that they should make up their mind as to what they wanted to be: a self-serving cooperative, or an outgoing Christian community. At this they all laughed and nodded their heads approvingly; the Kikuyus love a good debate and are generous when they think a telling point has been made.

The sequel was amusing. A venerable old lady stood up and berated the menfolk present. "The fathers" [there were three priests at the meeting] "have come to change you fellows and not the Gospel," she scolded.

Pope Paul VI and Pope John Paul II have insisted that the small Christian communities are *ecclesial*. So we are treating of units that are integral parts of the Church. In this way they differ from so many other groups and movements which enrich the Church with their specific charisms, yet are not regarded as ecclesial (integral, essential parts of the Church) in a full theological sense. Examples of these would be the various religious orders that arose in the course of history to redeem slaves from captivity. When the slave trade ended, their charism became irrelevant, so they too ceased.

In passing, I should like to say that we ought to avoid becoming fanatics for any group or movement, believing that our particular way is the *only* way.

Throughout history there has always existed a great variety of gifts in the Church. And so it will continue.

And what I say of other groups, I also say unreservedly of small Christian communities. We are saved in community. But not everyone, I think, is called to be a member of the Church's small ferment groups. God can relate people to one another in all sorts of ways: some will probably get the experience of relationship that they need in rather more enlarged assemblies, or in a different manner. Others will only be happy with the more intense living of community which the core group provides. Experience will tell.

Still, even though many may not be members of small Christian communities, their existence is necessary for all, because in one way or another they should touch the lives of all.

## Various Metaphors

Various metaphors are invoked to illumine the reality that is small community.

The small Christian community is the *tiny heart* that pumps out lifeblood to wider communities.

It is *salt:* a little salt gives savour to a great quantity of food; the group influences a great many people.

It is *light:* even a tiny light dispels an amazing amount of encroaching darkness. If you have ever sat in a dark Church where a little sanctuary lamp was fitfully flickering, you will have seen what is meant. As your eyes grew accustomed to the darkness, you will have noticed that its faint crimson glow may have searched out even the farthest recesses of the building. Thus the witness of a small group can reach far and wide.

A final helpful metaphor. Bishop Mwoleka of Rulenge, Tanzania speaks of the small Christian community as the *motor* that keeps the whole machine of the Ujamaa village ticking over. An Ujamaa village is one in which the inhabitants live and share as in a large family.

## The Ripple Effect

We have already spoken of the ripple effect of the small Christian community on a cosmic scale. The same is true of a limited environment. For argument sake, let us suppose there is a village, a street, or a rural area that has 500 people. Let us further suppose that there are 150 Christians in the place under consideration and that 20 belong to the core group. The influence of the 20 should, and in fact does, ripple out to the remaining Christians and to all the others as well.

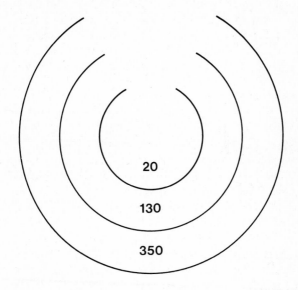

*Characteristics*

The small Christian community is an integral part of the Church. It ought therefore, at least when fully developed, to reflect all the essential characteristics of the universal Church. When it gets to the stage of being fully developed, a more accurate title for the group would in fact be, as explained in the Introduction, *small ecclesial community*.

But let us go to the characteristics. The members of the Church throughout the world *share the same faith*. So also do the members of the small Christian community, which is not just any agglomeration of persons but a gathering of those who believe in Jesus the Saviour of "the whole man and the whole of mankind" (Paul VI, *Populorum progressio,* par. 14).

*Christian love* is the most fundamental quality of the Church in all its manifestations: "By this all men will know you are my disciples, if you have love for one another" (Jn 13:35).

There was the case of a crotchety, disagreeable, yet destitute man on the verge of a great African city. The local Christian community came to his assistance. Among other things, the members built him a little house. Not long afterwards it was burned down.

Some participants of the group baulked at the idea of rebuilding it. After all, why help such a crotchety, disagreeable, thankless old sinner. There were even dark whisperings that he burned down the house himself.

One of the members protested at this attitude within the community: "Are we only going to help nice people then?" he asked. "Is that what Christianity is about?"

That of course is not what Christianity is about. It is about loving absolutely every person, even an enemy.

The Christian may burn with indignation at the rape of the environment, the threat of nuclear annihilation, or the exploitation of humans by humans; yet may not use any cause, however just, as an excuse to hate.

The little house, by the way, was rebuilt.

*Worship* is an essential element of the worldwide Church. It must also be found in its smallest unit. Indeed a group that is not centred on prayer, the Word of God, and the Eucharist has absolutely no chance of survival.

The Church is *missionary* (reaches out to people, especially to the needy) and *prophetic* (stands up for justice). We are a Church of servants. We shall have to dwell on these qualities in a later chapter. They will be found in the small Christian community.

To be *in communion with the pastors* of the Church is essential for every Christian group. Because we believe that today's pastors are the successors of the apostles, a small Christian community, to be fully recognised as such, should have the approval of the bishop. That the groups strive to stay close to their pastors and that the pastors help them to do so, I regard as a tremendous safeguard against sectarianism.

Finally, if the Church is not to stagnate, it must constantly renew itself. Frequent *renewal* is also vital for the small Christian community. This is achieved by means of evaluation. Every so often the community must evaluate every aspect of its life: spiritual, emotional, intellectual, and material.

Renewal is also facilitated by retreats, days of recollection, the meetings, courses, and social occasions.

These, then, are the essential elements of the Church in general and, consequently, of the small community. Just as all the ingredients of bread are to be found in a tiny piece of loaf, so ideally are all the ingredients of the universal Church to be found in its core group.


*Composition*

Since the small Christian community is the Church writ small, its members may differ regarding age, sex, calling, race, and so forth. As it is generally a neighbourhood group, the members usually come from the same socio-economic background. It is largely composed of laypersons and indeed its leaders are nearly always laity.

In Africa, there is a problem of participation for youth and women. Owing to traditions, young people often find it difficult to break into the communities in a meaningful way, while women, though accepted and frequently in the majority, do not seem to participate as fully as they might. Only rarely, for example, did I encounter a woman who had been chosen as leader.

The solution? Obviously, as Christians, we must work towards a situation where all categories of persons play their full part.

To help young people make a breakthrough, a possible strategy might be to bring youth and adult groups together once a month and thus break down barriers. This strategy might well be effective also in counteracting other divisive factors.

In African cities, the lines of division seem to blur and one finds articulate women and students in the small communities. Indeed there is the fear that the progressive youth may lose their traditional respect for the elders. More significant still, we find people of historically hostile tribes mingling in the same group: a marvellous Christian achievement.

*Commitment the Deciding Factor*

In the end it is not just the place or the persons that make small Christian community: it is the *commitment* or the total giving of themselves to Christ which the members undertake.

Yet this is too global and too vague an aim and

has to be made more precise in the particular environment.

In Northern Ireland, for instance, the aim might well be commitment to Christ in the non-violent pursuit of peace with justice. Then as a group progressed there, it would add sub-objectives which would make the overall one ever more precise and ever more relevant.

Commitment presupposes conversion. At some point the individuals in a community (it can only be as strong as its component parts) must have made a U-turn in their lives away from evil and towards God. Not that conversion is necessarily a sudden event: persons must work arduously throughout their lives, despite perhaps many falls, at growing in faith. In practice growing in faith means growing in love.


## Numbers in a Group

A final issue. How many members should a small Christian community have? Fifteen? Twenty? Forty? Rather than talk of numbers, let us talk of *participation:* there must be an adequate involvement of all the members in the meetings, apostolate, and life of the group. When a community gets so big that this becomes difficult, the members should consider dividing in order to form another one.

If the number goes above thirty, I feel it is getting somewhat big. Twenty I regard as small enough for all to play a vital role, yet large enough to produce the necessary leaders and ministries. Frankly, I am reluctant to lay down a hard-and-fast rule. Circumstances must decide. But this I would say: better five who give themselves totally than forty who shilly-shally.

If a group should be divided, I would strongly recommend that the participants agree. A forced division is not desirable and may not succeed.

# PART III

## HOW TO ORGANISE
## THE SMALL CHRISTIAN COMMUNITY

The guiding principle must be that organisation never becomes more important than persons: organisation exists for persons and not persons for organisation.

# 3

## STARTING THE SMALL CHRISTIAN COMMUNITY

There is no fixed pattern or magical formula for commencing a small Christian community. *You must start from where you are*. This means that you must take local circumstances very much into account. Founding a group, for example, in an area where there is a long history of the traditional parish is one thing; doing so where the Church is breaking new ground quite another.

It is best to develop small community around people who have some *experience of living and working together*. There will most certainly be a *common interest* such as social problems to solve or a desire for togetherness. The following are examples of groups that have gone on to become small Christian communities:

—prayer, charismatic, and catechetical groupings
—close neighbours
—migrants
—discussion and problem-solving groups

In Africa it has often been:

—a core of the extended family
—a nucleus of village or outstation
—a group of the newly baptized

Where ordinary human cohesion is wanting, you cannot move to Christian community. The second storey cannot be put on a house until the first is securely in place. So if in a situation there is isolation and alienation, our first preoccupation must be to foster human relationships, for friendship is at the heart of community. I do not mean that everything has to drip with sentiment. What I have in mind is mature persons overcoming the inevitable differences, caused by temperament and circumstances, to put into practice effectively the biblical injunctions to bear one another's burdens (Galatians 6:2) and to do all their work in love (1 Corinthians 16:14).

*Process* is a major factor in the growth of a community. We must accept the participants as they are, yet challenge them to grow, and we must strive to create the conditions that favour growth. There is a gradualness in all this and we must not expect people to run before they have even begun to walk.

To respect process is merely to follow the pattern of God's action in our own regard.

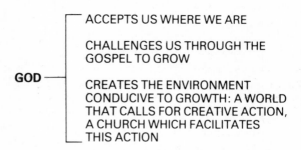

**GOD** —

ACCEPTS US WHERE WE ARE

CHALLENGES US THROUGH THE GOSPEL TO GROW

CREATES THE ENVIRONMENT CONDUCIVE TO GROWTH: A WORLD THAT CALLS FOR CREATIVE ACTION, A CHURCH WHICH FACILITATES THIS ACTION

There are two things which must be impressed upon the members from the outset. Firstly they are never meant to be an élite who consider themselves superior to others; the good Lord is calling them to service, not to conceit. Secondly they will not be perfect. The euphoria which nearly always accompanies the commencement of a small community may lead people into thinking that they are the ideal group. Problems soon surface. They find that we do not change so suddenly after all and harmony has to be struggled for with perseverance.

Naturally not all the features of the small Christian community will be found in a group at the start: we have to work towards that point. It is an absorbing journey.

## Formation

Formation is of the utmost importance and ought to begin with the commencement of a group and never cease throughout its whole life. And we are treating of formation in its fullest sense: spiritual, intellectual, and human.

Now much formation comes through dialogue at meetings and, for that matter, through ordinary conversation. With time, however, the members of a community usually request a more formalised approach as well. As a result of encounters and discussions in their places of study or work, they may, for example, realise their deficiencies regarding the Bible or religious knowledge and ask for a solid grounding in the one or the other. These are opportunities for the competent person to step in and meet a praiseworthy need. The priest has an important role to play here. Among the means for achieving this are courses, seminars, retreats, and days of recollection.

I was once present while a group which had been in existence several years, despite ups and downs, were trying to decide the chief reason for their perseverance. They were unanimous: it was the formation they had received and were still receiving.

*Apostolate (Work)*

Right from the outset, too, the need for the community to *do* something ought to be emphasised: "faith apart from works is dead" (James 2:26).

Actually there is an enormous *do barrier,* whose proportions are often underestimated, between talk and action. That the action meet a real-life need is also important. It must not be a case of pastoral basketmaking which serves no purpose other than to satisfy the one who is doing it.

Sometimes there are persons who protest that they are so absorbed by their normal duties that they can find no time to do anything for God. There is a misconception here: the separation of religion and life. The apostolate is not necessarily taking on extra chores: primarily it is a question of doing in Christ what one is already committed to do because of one's career. I have found this misconception deep-rooted in some Irish groups.

The hospital, for example, is the doctor's place of action. Through his dedication, patience, and kindness he will strive to make Christ present in the hospital ward. In addition he will place his skill at the service of his community. If a neighbour is sick, he will call and see whether there may be something he can do.

The student's first concern will be his place of education. He will do what he can to foster the Kingdom of God there. Then, like the doctor, he will put his ability at the service of his neighbourhood. Maybe there is a child living nearby who needs a little extra coaching in mathematics.

The factory-worker will try to be another Christ on the shop floor and will not lose sight of fellow-workers outside the plant.

This is the basic approach. In practice, of course, generous people find time to do all kinds of extra tasks, such as teaching catechism, working for youth, and helping the handicapped. If members work in teams or if a whole community addresses itself to a common task, the unified endeavour involved binds the members firmly together.

## An Instrument for True Development

The small Christian community, quite apart from the faith dimension, is an excellent instrument for true integral development. Development is above all a matter of enhancing *persons,* a matter of getting people to *think, speak,* and *act,* however humbly, on their own behalf.

Persons or countries cannot *be* developed; they must *develop* themselves. Sympathisers can help the process, but it is those involved who must see it through. It is not enough that someone becomes the voice of the voiceless. The voiceless must find their own voice.

The Third World is a graveyard of elaborate projects which outsiders felt would be good for the resident populations. In reality they were destined to fail because the locals were neither involved in, nor consulted regarding them. And, in any case, the sophistication of the works was far beyond local capabilities. One of the mistakes of recent decades was the belief that books, buildings, machines, and money would improve the lives of the people while structures that favoured privileged minorities were left intact.

On the other hand, I have seen simple bush schools and clinics, which were built by local people, being well looked after. The difference was that these schools and clinics belonged to the people.

When I come in contact with a group for the first time, there are two questions in my mind. One, certainly, is whether the participants are *doing* something necessary and practical and not just tracing aerial circles round some Scripture passage without ever coming down to earth.

The other preoccupation concerns whether the group is working to stay close to its pastors. This does not entail sacrificing its prophetic character.

I feel worried when a community is either other-worldly or sectarian.

# 4

## HOW THE SMALL CHRISTIAN COMMUNITY DEVELOPS

A development often takes place in the life of the small Christian community that can be compared to the stages of human growth.

There is a period at the beginning which we might liken to *childhood*. This is a time of good-feeling when new friends are made and old ones seem to draw still closer. It is a moment of euphoria; the Lord seems to be nourishing the group on milk. Alas, this passes all too soon.

The next stage is the *adolescent* one. And now it often begins to look as though the whole world is falling apart. Where all was sweetness and light, problems now abound: jealousies, ambitions, tangled emotions, gossip, and cliques. Actually what is happening is that the community is passing through a period of painful but inevitable growth.

Only faith can carry the core group through this crisis. The motivation must be got right: the initiator of the particular small community ought to insist that the members come to the group primarily in search of Christ and that they must cling for support to the Eucharist, prayer, and the Word of God. A community thus sustained will not be undone by troubles arising from within or without its membership.

And there are other helpful factors: talking things

through, being busy on behalf of others, and being confirmed in faith and unity by an interested priest.

In those parts of the world where a sense of community has been weakened or lost, a reduced community can cease to exist at the adolescent stage. On running into difficulties, the participants give up rather too easily, not realising that community is like marriage: after the honeymoon the couple have to work hard at the relationship if it is to be successful. The true gold of small Christian community will not be found on the surface. To discover it we must dig hard and deep.

I have seen groups which, by means of regular evaluation from the start, have forestalled or blunted the edge of problems related to the adolescent phase.

Once past the turmoil of adolescence, the little community reaches maturity. Problems persist, of course, yet they do not unduly upset the members, and there is a greater ability to cope.

In the nature of things, I suppose old age is more prone to intolerance, closemindedness, and irrelevance than youth. The small Christian community too, if not extremely careful to cultivate the opposing virtues, may with time manifest signs of aging.

The development of small Christian community does not have to follow the foregoing clearcut stages. Indeed the stages are not usually all that clearcut. Often enough, however, the groups trace a path that somewhat reflects the pattern set out here.

# 5

## HOW TO COORDINATE THE SMALL CHRISTIAN COMMUNITY

Leadership in a community-type Church is above all the ability to *coordinate*. Thus the effective leader in a small Christian community is not one who is out ahead pulling people after her, or behind pushing people onwards; rather the leader is one who walks shoulder to shoulder with the others and encourages and coordinates their efforts to go forward of their own accord. (From this point on, in fact, when I refer to coordinators, I am thinking in terms of leaders.)

Generally speaking these leaders are laity. A religious or priest may initiate a group, but will gradually put its coordination in lay hands.

*Qualities of the Good Coordinator*

First of all let us recall the qualities stressed by John Paul II. The Holy Father urges that lay-animators be *in communion* with their pastors, be *prepared* in the faith, and be of *exemplary* life.

I once asked a long-surviving group what quality they most looked for in their coordinators; they were unanimous: constancy. It is of the utmost importance that the leader be responsible and predictable, an unalterable point of reference.

I have a small personal experience which illustrates this. In the Latin American *barrio* where I worked, it was announced at Sunday Masses that there would be sessions for youth every Thursday at 8 p.m. to treat of teenage problems.

No one appeared the first Thursday and I just sat reading a book.

The second Thursday some teenagers looked at me gingerly through the window.

It was the third occasion that Jorge, René, and Mauro trickled in. And it all began from there: lively weekly sessions with the room chock full of teenagers, a well-attended Youth Mass every Sunday evening, and, eventually, groups of young leaders which persist to this day. I was glad that I did not lose heart at the beginning.

Furthermore, a coordinator has to encourage *co-operation*. In a true team there will be no rigid demarcations; none of the spirit of "This is my area, and dare anyone interfere!" Each one must be interested in and know what the others do, lend a hand when necessary, even be ready to fill in for others.

If a defender falls in a hockey match, for example, and an attacker is racing unimpeded towards goal, the nearest other defender does her utmost to cover up. She will not stand idly by saying that it isn't her job. Or, when opportune, a back will often sally up into the forward line and score a brilliant goal!

The good leader must be *skilled in dialogue*. As well as speaking, this involves being able truly to *listen:* listen to the extent of being able to get into the shoes of another person to see what exactly moves that person. Skill in dialogue also means being adept at summarising and giving shape to discussions, and chivying people towards decision and action.

*Respecting process* is again a feature of good leadership: accepting persons where they are, challenging them to growth, and trying to create the conditions favourable to growth. It is also most important for the leader to know when and in what measure to let go of responsibility as she eases herself out of coordination.

Finally the effective coordinator will know how to *encourage* members and, without being unrealistic about defects and problems, will highlight the positive.

In Sierra Leone I once saw a cuddly pet cat that had been run over; whether by a certain priest or a certain sister was hotly debated! The cat at any rate was very dead. The vultures were down in a trice to dismember and devour it. And I thought to myself: those vultures were flying majestically, high above the earth, high above the lush green of the bush, the waving tropical palms, the colourful shrubs and flowers, the sparkling waterfalls and rivers, the rolling hills ... Yet amid all that splendour they only had eyes for a lifeless animal. We too can become so obsessed with the defective that we miss the wholesome.

*Planned and Emergent Coordinators*

There are *planned and emergent* coordinators. To illustrate, I shall take a process whereby small Christian communities are sometimes formed. Key persons (priests, religious, and laity) are given the know-how about establishing communities. These are your planned leaders.

Naturally the planned person has to be responsible for the group for quite a time until coordinators emerge and are formed from among the members themselves. This will of course mean involving the participants in the meetings and work of the community, so that they get ample opportunities to develop their talents. As people emerge, the planned leader will phase herself out.

Instead of having one coordinator, there is now a tendency to have *a coordinating team* of about three. Thus the principle of community is seen at work even in the management of the group.

A solitary coordinator can easily begin to develop a proprietary attitude and start talking of "my community". Besides, others should be given a chance to prove and develop their potential. Experience has led many to change their leaders with relative frequency.

There are sometimes practical reasons too that counsel the choice of a team rather than of an individual. In many places, for instance, the members of the small Christian communities do shift-work in factories or mines, so one or other of the coordinators may be in the factory or down the mine while the meeting is in session.

## Duties of a Coordinator

Coordinators perform a variety of tasks such as the following: they summon and direct meetings, conduct celebrations of the Word, lead prayer, distribute communion, and organise teams to be responsible for the various activities of the group.

## Ministries

Within the group God also raises up persons with the ministries or charisms that the particular community requires. Often enough a charism is what we might describe as an individual's forte. An abiding quality. Thus one might have a marked ability for prayer, interpreting the Bible, music, or teaching catechism; still another for working with youth or helping the sick and the aged. I knew a young man who did enormous good by being a clown for Christ.

Need I add here that we are not speaking of ministry in the strict sense, that is of ministry such as diaconate or priesthood which come with ordination. There is no question of ordination where the ministries we refer to are concerned.

The coordinators ought to encourage the members to use their gifts for the good of the group and its apostolate. Come to think of it, coordination is itself a key ministry.

## Authority

It is vital that the coordinators and members of a small Christian community have the correct concept of authority. Jesus turns the worldly notion of authority on its head. Authority, he tells us, is for *service,* not for dominance: "You know that the rulers of the Gentiles lord it over them, and their great men exercise authority over them. It shall not be so among you; but whoever would be great among you must be your servant, and whoever would be first among you must be your slave; even as the Son of Man came not to be served but to serve, and to give his life as a ransom for many" (Matthew 20:25-28).

To further make his point, Christ leaves us the abiding image of himself washing the feet of his disciples.

In a talk given at the Catholic University of São Paulo, September 1981, Bishop Pedro Casaldáliga of São Felix had this to say: "Every year I sit down and plan for our diocese together with my ordinary lay-people. I am no more or no less than anyone else there. We are brothers and sisters in Christ. The fact that I am a bishop is a service which I must give to the community."

In a few brief sentences Dom Pedro has captured the fresh vision of Church which is growing among the people of God. These words are quickly read, yet staggering in their implications.

Then there was the old man Josiah in Kenya. He belonged to a thriving small Christian community.

"What is the work of the priest in your community, Josiah?" I enquired.

"The father", he answered, "is our friend, our guide. When we go the wrong road, he brings us back. But he is not the one who *do*. We must *do*."

His vision I like. There is the realisation that the laity are the Church just as much as are the clergy.

*Dialogue*

The word *dialogue* occurs about fifty times in the Council documents, so presumably the Holy Spirit was trying to tell us something of its importance. Pope Paul VI says that it is through "trustful dialogue" in a community that we discover God's will for the group (*Evangelica testificatio*, 25). This of course implies an honest, objective search for truth. It would be quite wrong for me, however convinced I might be, to force my opinion on a community or so to manipulate matters that my view prevails.

Dialogue is that ability to sit down and calmly thrash things out together like friends. It involves a deep listening process. Really it is not something we do with our ears, tongues, facial expressions, or gestures so much as with our whole being.

So a core group carries out its affairs on a basis of consensus through dialogue. In such an environment, however, it is important that a prophetic voice be not lost. The community will be carefully discerning and sincerely respectful of those rare voices (and lives) that shake our complacency; those voices may well point to the paths of the future.


*Role of the Bishop*

The bishop, as you would expect, plays a key role in the small Christian communities. He is the *sign of unity* who:

—coordinates and animates in God's name
—serves
—teaches
—guides
—governs (always in a context of service)
—approves of
—and relates, not only small Christian communities, but Christian communities of all kinds (small, area, parish, diocese) to one another and to the Church at large.

His is a role that finds its inspiration in The Constitution on the Church:

> ". . . the bishops received the charge of the community, presiding in God's stead over the flock of which they are the shepherds in that they are teachers of doctrine, ministers of sacred worship and holders of office in government." (n. 20)

The bishop cannot possibly do his task alone. He needs his *helpers,* the priests and deacons. In fact there was a far greater proportion of bishops to faithful in the early Church than there is today. They were, consequently, deeply enmeshed in the daily details of the lives of their people. The shepherd in time became sadly distanced, owing to administrative burdens, from his flock. Yet the intermediary, though necessary, cannot supply for the lack of direct contact.

Briefly then the priest and deacon, as helpers, render the core groups similar services to those of the bishop himself.

Pastors who are accustomed to the traditional Church sometimes feel threatened by the small communities. They believe that their influence will somehow be diminished. Those who have made the leap, however, would assure them that the truth is quite the contrary. Indeed it is only when the laity play their role fully that the pastors discover their true identity and fulfilment. The clergy and the laity are not opposing forces. They beautifully complement each other.

There are other advantages. I met a New Mexican priest who told me what an utterly harried man he was until he initiated the core groups. Now that they are well under way, he can find adequate time for reading and reflection. When hard cases arise in the parish, he is not alone. By merely lifting the phone, he can set a whole support network in operation.

### The Parish and the Small Christian Communities

What can happen as the small Christian communities multiply in a parish is that they transform it into a *communion of communities*.

The *parochial house* can be the *coordinating centre* for small communities and indeed for all groups in the parish.

It can also be an effective *centre of service*. In many areas, for example, there will be sent out to all the communities materials for such varied events as: Christmas novena, Easter preparation, Bible-study months. Diocesan and other pastoral centres often render a similar service.

As a matter of fact, the small Christian communities can and do provide an excellent *network for the catechesis* of both youth and adults.

And, if true communication is ordinary people relating to each other in a personal and intimate way, surely the groups are among the best possible forums for doing this. Bombarding by vested interests in the media is at best manipulation and at worst brainwashing. It can lead to masses of people being submerged in blissful unawareness and enslaved by false values.

One wonders even about the effectiveness of the paltry spots devoted to religion in the mass media. Could it be that the religious programme serves only to legitimise the ceaseless flow of consumerism? Give it an air of respectability? After all, if you put a spoonful of even the most exquisite wine into a large cistern of water, it emerges indistinguishable from water.

Surely communication is dialogue with one another in a search for the truth so that the truth can be done. Is not this best achieved in modest uncomplicated ways? Has not communication been made the preserve of the moguls of science, technology, and big business? Indeed has not communication itself become big, prepackaged business? Is the Word of God not smothered when spoken amid a welter of highly commercial programmes? These questions really do need thinking out.


*The Part of the Religious Community*

Religious orders have a tradition and experience of community living that oftentimes span centuries.

They have much to share with the groups now forming. They indeed ought to be good examples of what is worthwhile in community.

Religious too can be effective apostles in the spreading of small Christian communities. This has been particularly true of sisters who frequently are not as circumscribed as priests by present Church structures.

*Relating Small Christian Community*
*to the Universal Church*

To relate small Christian community to the universal Church, we recall our earlier scheme:

Note again that the community model prevails through all phases.

The foregoing is one way in which a community-type Church can express itself. It has the decided advantage of starting from where we are and developing from what already exists.

## The Family

The well-being of all society depends enormously on the health of the family. And what can be said of all society can be said equally of the Church. Good Christian families provide worthy members of the Church and of its small communities. The small Christian communities in their turn promote the stability of the family.

## Fresh Possibilities

There are of course fresh possibilities. At the Curia of the Archdiocese of Vitoria, Espiritu Santo, Brazil, their approach was explained to me as follows. At the centre there is the group of some 50 persons. Present at their meetings owing to work and other circumstances, one usually finds about 30. Within the sphere of influence of this small community there are about 200 persons who frequently rally round it for specific purposes: celebration of the Eucharist, for example, or a meeting in connection with problems. Starting from this small Christian community, the total organisation in the Archdiocese goes like this:

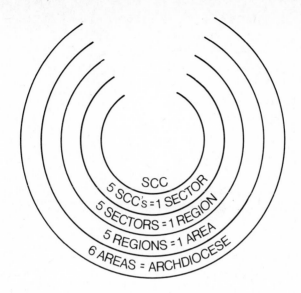

SCC
5 SCC's = 1 SECTOR
5 SECTORS = 1 REGION
5 REGIONS = 1 AREA
6 AREAS = ARCHDIOCESE

At all phases there is a coordinating body with a preponderance of lay representation. The final body is the Archdiocesan Assembly. In this assembly there are also representatives from the flourishing workers' movement and from the youth groups.

In addition to the various coordinating groups, there are Archdiocesan General Assemblies, which seek to bring the small Christian communities together in force, so as to give them a sense of unity and solidarity. To achieve this there are for example congresses or joint Easter celebrations.

Yet, despite this novel approach, I noted as I went about the city that the traditional parish service was available for those who wished. While something new was growing, the old was receding with, I imagine, a minimum of confrontation and pain.

## Zoning

Sometimes a parish is zoned into, let us say, twenty divisions, which are then considered to be twenty small Christian communities. The problem here is that in zoning we may unwittingly cut across natural human and Christian groupings:

On the other hand, groups confined to arbitrarily designated sectors round a Nairobi factory seemed to flourish. The sectors, called "phases", are well-defined. In that sense they are, I suppose, comparable to rural villages. Zoning, therefore, will depend very much on local circumstances.

It may be wise, because of the danger of splitting spontaneous groupings, to simply float the idea of forming small Christian communities and allow people to find the rallying points with which they feel most comfortable. Presumably these will be in their own neighbourhoods. There is no point in uprooting persons from where God has planted them and wants them to grow.

# 6

## MEETINGS OF THE SMALL CHRISTIAN COMMUNITY

There are four staple components in the group meeting. These are:

The Bible
Community
Reality
Worship

It is when we reflect upon the Bible in community and relate our reflections to real life and its problems in an atmosphere of prayer that we have a formula for progress.

The meeting must be *functional,* that is, it must respond to a real need. One night the community may be planning or evaluating its work, and the meeting is devoted to that particular task. Next time the session could be devoted to examining a problem.

The need of the moment normally decides the shape of the session: there ought to be no rigid pattern. This does not mean that meetings are unplanned. Quite the contrary. In fact preparation has to be more thorough than when there is a regular format. Usually at the end of a meeting the members decide the subject for the next.

A group, of course, may want to have a few on-going themes for those inevitable moments when nothing of urgency presents itself. A group I know have decided to go systematically through St Mark's Gospel and a document of Vatican II.

When we speak of meetings, we are usually referring to formal gatherings. Yet our lives are made up of rather more relaxed encounters: coming across friends, a game of cards, study groups, meetings to prepare for, or celebrate, the sacraments, cultural or religious functions, outings, holidays, and pilgrimages. All of these can help enormously in forging community. We should be aware of this.

*Meetings Proper*

We shall now deal with the small Christian community meeting proper (the word *formal* does not fit). Since the group is a cell of the Church and reflects its varied life, it is obvious that the meeting will show that variety.

\*      \*      \*

(a) There is the *worship* session: devoted entirely to prayer, the Eucharist, the Word, or reconciliation. Since the groups are composed not of angels but of imperfect humans, there will always be need for a spirit of reconciliation among the participants. If we were perfect, we would not hurt each other. As we are not, we do so even without meaning to.

Sample worship session (reconciliation):

(1) There is dialogue regarding misunderstandings.

(2) Does Scripture shed any light on the situation. There follows reflection and discussion.

(3) Prayer now takes place. People express their sorrow.

(4) The participants decide on practical steps to avoid misunderstandings in the future.

(5) A sign of peace may terminate the session.

Note the presence of the Bible, community, reality, and prayer. Note too that music and song will enliven any meeting.

## Use of the Bible

The Bible is the salvation story of the Jewish people and of the early Christians of varying origins. Their story has been preserved for us as the inspired written Word of God. We must not, however, use the Bible in a vacuum while failing to read our own 'Bible' in the events of our daily lives. When reading the sacred Scriptures, therefore, we should do so in a way that is life-related.

## The Eucharist

The Eucharist is an occasion in which we celebrate our whole lives. In a Brazilian community before Mass began, I found people saying what it was they wished to celebrate since last coming together: the birth of a child, the kindness of some neighbour the struggle for justice, and their many martyrs.

A friend told me of a Mass he saw in the São Felix area of the same country. Very much part of the liturgy were the items that featured.in the lives of the fisherfolk there: the nets and the baskets of fish. And the bishop instead of using the unfamiliar shep-

61

herd's staff, carried the familiar fisherman's oar.

In Africa I have known Masses that pulse with the enthusiasm of the participants. The sound of drumming and singing fills the air, and the offertory includes the produce of the local fields.

The Eucharist above all celebrates the harmony that exists in the small Christian community. It is a sign of that harmony. And it re-inforces the co-hesion of the group. Should a community be divided, though, it does not heal this rift as if by magic.

\*   \*   \*

(b) The *prophetic meeting* is yet another possibility. This would involve announcing and celebrating justice and denouncing injustice. I will use an example from an area where women are, sadly, second-class citizens. A lady who in fact had a doctorate said that, simply because she was a woman, her opinion was neither sought nor esteemed by men, some of whom could barely read or write.

(1) The group in question was reading John 4, the story of the woman at the well.

(2) Noting Jesus' attitude of deep respect for the Samaritan women, whom he treated as a *person* despite the lowly position of women in Jewish society, the community got into an animated discussion on the status of women in their environment ... men deeply questioned ...

(3) Spontaneous prayer

(4) Practical decisions ... men took to helping with domestic chores!

To give some idea of the change involved in men doing those chores in that particular culture, one would have to conjure up an image of Superman washing diapers.

*     *     *

(c) There are *ecumenical sessions* where Protestants and Catholics come together on occasions to pray or plan a common activity. If it is a question of filling potholes, well, there is no such thing as a Catholic or a Protestant pothole, only potholes. When persons of different denominations can join together in prayer and in doing something practical for their environmental or social betterment, it is surely a wonderful testimony to unity. This has been done to good effect in Latin America where Catholics and Protestants have stood shoulder to shoulder in life and, indeed, in death. A good example would be the solidarity of the Evangelical Methodist Church of Bolivia, guided by its bishop, Mortimer Arias, with the Catholic Church in the struggle for liberation.

I have been dealing with the small Christian community in a Catholic context. I have not touched on a similar tendency among other denominations, simply because I lack sufficient experience in the matter.

For the same reason I have not touched upon experiments at small Christian community of mixed denominations. One can readily see the witness potential of such groups, especially when they bridge a great divide as they would do, for example, in Northern Ireland.

Such experience as I do have of groups composed of persons of different Christian denominations makes me realise that the mixing in community of people who are not well-grounded in their own particular belief is a recipe for confusion.

But work for Christian unity is of the utmost importance. One of the last and most urgent prayers of Christ was that we might be one (John 17:21), and it is imperative that we settle on the best strategies to achieve this.

For my part I have been able to travel far with Protestants, and indeed with persons of religions other than Christian, who will join hands with me in working for a world that is more just, and better reflects the face of God. There are those who work hard for a humane world and profess no religion at all. They merit cooperation.

It is also possible to organize meetings for encounters with non-Christian faith. After all, the Moslems and ourselves do worship the same God. And there are no Moslem potholes either.

\* \* \*

(d) *Commitment* (total giving) being the soul of community, there will have t be sessions to treat of this.

\* \* \*

(e) There will have to be meetings to *plan* and *evaluate*.

\* \* \*

(f) Finally there are encounters simply to help the members of a small community *to get to know* each other better.

Such a meeting could follow this format:
(1) Each member relates the happiest or saddest experience of his/her life and tries to show something at least of how he/she feels.

(When we unveil our feelings others understand us more). Then there will be reflection
and dialogue.
(2) Can Scripture illuminate the situation?
Reflection on the Word of God.
(3) Prayer
(4) Evaluation of the experience. What practical
implications has it for our lives?

\*    \*    \*

*The Word of God, Prayer, and the Eucharist*

If a small community is not to fall apart, then the
Word, prayer, and the Eucharist must firmly
support it. The Word and prayer must find their
way into every session, and Mass will hopefully be a
frequent feature. Meetings normally last two hours.
If the whole gathering is not devoted to the Word of
God, prayer, or the Eucharist, I would suggest
that twenty minutes to half-an-hour be set aside at
the end for explicit worship.

I am not saying that planning or evaluation, or
any such activity is not prayer. Obviously there is
no dividing line between prayer and non-prayer in a
life dedicated to God. Nonetheless explicit worship
ought to be a part of every session, even though
some business may have to be postponed until a
subsequent meeting.

Some have found *exercises* helpful in promoting
the community process, especially in the first couple
of years of a group's life. I have in mind those types
of exercises, frequently simple and homemade, that
provoke discussion about real life. In Africa, for example, I saw simple drama (sketches) used to great
effect.

Exercises I believe should be used with great sensitivity and care. I have serious reservations about dynamics that do not just challenge, but upset, people. Often badly. This is especially true if the community in question has neither the commitment nor competence to pick up the pieces when some one is shattered.

In Antoine de Saint-Exupery's *The Little Prince*, the Fox reminds us that we are responsible for what we tame. By taming is meant establishing relationships. We should not establish a relationship with someone and then behave as if this had never been done.

A lonely lady in a great city went to a prayer meeting seeking support. She was received most warmly by the participants and the whole experience proved a great uplift for her. Yet once the meeting was over, the people disappeared quickly to carry on with their busy lives and she was more lonely than ever. They did not prove responsible for what they tamed.

*Resource Material*

A good Bible with illustrations and explanations such as the *Jerusalem Bible* or the *New American Bible* will be of enormous help to a group. Commentaries on sacred Scriptures will also prove invaluable. Pastors and resource persons must strive to open up the treasures of the Bible for their communities.

Books with suitable or adaptable exercises can be helpful. And stories too can provide interesting material.*

*cf. Further Reading (p. 131 ff) for examples of books that may serve as resource material.

## Place

Any place that is simple and friendly will be adequate for meetings of the community. A home would be ideal. And a household which thus accommodates a group benefits from the openness. A cup of tea or coffee (never anything lavish) after a session can add warmth to an occasion. In some parts of the world, indeed, families are so desperately poor that providing even a cup of tea or coffee proves a hardship.

Meetings are usually held once a week. There may be circumstances, however, which make this extremely difficult. In this case people can only do the best they can.

# 7

## PASTORAL PLANNING IN THE SMALL CHRISTIAN COMMUNITY

Rather too often one finds small Christian communities, even parishes, dioceses, or religious congregations which suffer from not having any pastoral plan. The result can be a great deal of well-intentioned, yet sometimes aimless, or even mistaken, activity. Another result can be an extremely frustrated laity because priorities seem to change with every new pastor. Not unreasonably, they complain about lack of continuity.

If there is to be continuity in pastoral situations, two things are required: a common plan and good involved lay leaders. Then, no matter who comes or goes, there will be no serious dislocations on the pastoral scene.

Normally small Christian communities make a plan of action that responds to some seemingly obvious needs in their area. I have, however, occasionally met some well-established groups that have done some quite methodic planning. I shall outline a method for doing this which in practice I found satisfactory.

*Know the Reality*

There can be no question of valid pastoral planning until we know our local situation through and through. To do this we must be methodical. We can in fact live in a place and still not know it well.

The method I have in mind has a definite pattern:
—situating oneself
—the approadh
—first encounter
—second encounter
—dissection of problems
—analysis of system
—the global view
—the standpoint of the Church
—planning

## Situating Oneself

There must be a preliminary investigation which should assist the community to get to know their area better: boundaries, hills and hollows (topography); rivers, ditches, and ponds (hydrography); climate; electricity, water supplies, roads and buses (infrastructure and communications); living conditions, races, customs, and places of assembly (social factors).

The results of this initial enquiry are written up and a sketch drawn of the locality.

Should the small Christian community be able to enlist expert help with this and succeeding phases of the study, well and good. If not, they must do the best they can with their own resources. By expert help I mean a person or persons experienced in facilitating this kind of study.

## The Approach

Here the members of the small community will talk in earnest with the ordinary people so as to investigate a variety of areas: the family, working conditions, cultural manifestations, predominant sicknesses, political involvement, and religious practices. They then draw up a first version of a group of area problems.

## First Encounter

Up to this point it is quite possible that the investigating team may have been putting its own slant on all its findings. This bias must be eliminated. In the previous stage the team will have had close contact with certain of the residents. This group is now enlarged and a meeting held. The participants should be confronted with the preliminary list of problems. Their opinions should be sought, and they should be urged to reflect deeply.

The coordinator of the gathering has to get beyond the point where people are telling the investigators what they think they want to hear.

When we carried out this examination in our South American *barrio,* it seemed at first that the genuine worry of the people was to provide a steeple for the Church — in an area where there was malnutrition, astronomical unemployment, ignorance, prostitution, and so on. The people felt that I, the priest, would want a steeple. Prolonged dialogue showed that a steeple was among the least of their felt needs.

And the team must pay close attention to any

argument that breaks out in the course of conversation. Much can be learned from arguments.

This meeting should provide a second more authentic version of a list of problems.


## The Second Encounter

In a further effort to eliminate all subjective colouring, the core group will summon a second encounter. There should be about sixty persons present, a good cross-section of the local community. Once again the animating team will provoke questions and discussions regarding the problem-situation. The assembly may be split into groups for this work and ideas may be pooled in a plenary session.

Generally, significant changes result from this meeting. Items are dropped, profound additions are made, and a far more reliable catalogue of difficulties is produced. *Generative problems*, that is *those problems which cause several others*, are also identified.


## Dissection of Problems

By now, the small Christian community ought to understand the area and have a reasonably reliable list of problems and generative problems. Nevertheless something more is needed. The members now must mull over the *root causes* of the difficulties they have met.

## Analysis of the System

The pondering ought to be deep and extensive. Eventually it should bring the group face to face with the evils of the system in which they live: it should expose values, attitudes, and actions that are poisoned in their sources.

## The Global View

The study group may even take a look beyond the area in question. They will probably find that the evils which prevail there are, allowances being made for local nuances, to be met with in neighbouring regions, in the country at large and, indeed, throughout the world. In short, the menacing octopus of sin curls its constricting tentacles round the entire globe.

## The Standpoint of the Church

Once the reality is analysed, it will be obvious that it has socio-economic, political, and religious dimensions. These factors must now be examined in the light of *the Bible, the teaching of the Church,* and in the light of *local Church history.* To plan pastorally, that is in a Church-related way, we simply must take the standpoint of the Church into account.

## Planning

At this stage of the investigation, the community

is deeply involved in a conscientising process. They will have become greatly aware of their own reality. They will have realised that humans feel a mysterious call to growth. They will have realized that the world not only provides food for the body but also helps us to mature as complete persons. They will have realised that, if people are to control their environment and cope with their situation, they must cooperate closely with one another. They may even have realised that it is in acting thus that humankind will become authors of their own history and cease to be simply passive victims of circumstance.

Having discovered the reality and key problems of their area, the community will now feel impelled to do something about the situation. They are ready to plan. There follows a list of practical norms for such planning:

(1) start from knowledge of the reality;
(2) discover the key problems;
(3) realise what people are capable of;
(4) feel a need for organisation;
(5) decide on activities to set a process of change in motion;
(6) decide objectives and the appropriate means to achieve them;
(7) programme activities precisely (times and places);
(8) commit ourselves;
(9) go into action; and
(10) evaluate periodically.

*Conscientisation*

All the foregoing steps combine to produce a process of *conscientisation*. Conscientisation is not simply a raising of consciousness or a sharpening of awareness in a theoretical fashion. It is a *gradual,* often painstaking, awakening of consciousness and sharpening of awareness resulting from an action/reflection approach to life. The concern is to become aware so that we may *do* something, especially for those people whom the world pushes aside.

An example may help. There was a small Christian community which decided to give the poorest children of its area a little present for a festive occasion.

Reflecting on this action at their weekly meeting, the members thought it went well. One person remarked on the reaction of the children's parents, however. They looked on rather sadly.

None too quickly, it dawned on them that maybe the parents were humiliated because they themselves were not giving their own children the presents.

So next time round, the parents were given the gifts and then went on to present them to their offspring as coming from themselves.

In their next meeting, the group agreed that this proved much more successful. But then someone wondered why it was that those parents could not afford even a small gift for their own children.

By dint of action and reflection the community was getting to the heart of the social problem.

*The Kingdom*

The ultimate goal of all our striving is to establish

the Kingdom of God here on earth: the Kingdom of
God which is:

a kingdom of truth and life,

a kingdom of holiness and grace

a kingdom of justice, peace, and love,

(Preface for the Feast of Christ the King.)
If we believe in Christ and our fellow humans, we
must believe that this is possible, even if it has never
been achieved in the whole history of the world and
will be perfectly achieved only in the hereafter.

# PART IV

---

# YOUTH TO YOUTH

# 8

## THE YOUTH APOSTOLATE

The youth apostolate is closely related to the small Christian community. The youth group proper is an excellent training ground for the community. Then again, many young people, some pertaining to youth groups and some not form a great and influential part of the membership of the small Christian communities.

Virtually all of what has been said in previous chapters is relevant for youth groups. I shall merely add some considerations which may be of help.

*Specific youth groups?*

Should young people have their own specific youth groups apart from adult communities? Does the gathering of youth in clubs simply hive them off from the adult community in unchristian ghettos? It is obviously a danger.

Ultimately, of course, young people must answer this question for themselves. My own feeling, however, is that youth have their own special needs that are best served in the specific youth group provided that it remains *open* to adult groupings and the wider Christian and human communities. And, incidentally, it makes less and less sense today not to relate to the parents of the teenagers whom we serve.

But while bearing all this in mind, I should like to insist that the presence of the young in the small Christian community as well is necessary for its life. They in a special way can be open to change. And if it is true that at times they are a little hard on the accelerator, well, they balance out for the adults who are often heavy-footed with the brake.

Who exactly classify as youth? A question that never really bothered me until in a certain part of Africa I discovered some persons who were members of the Catholic youth organisation, and proudly wore its uniform, at sixty. This surely taxed even a most generous stretch of the imagination.

In my experience, youth groups divide roughly into early teens, late teens, and early twenties. Twenty-five would be about the upper limit.

## Youth the Apostles of Youth

Vatican II says: "The young should become the first apostles of the young, in direct contact with them, exercising the apostolate by themselves among themselves, taking account of their social environment" (Decree on the Apostolate of the Laity, 12).

There is a deep implication here. If the young are the *first* (not the only) apostles of their peers, then it is of *the utmost importance* to prepare youth leaders in groups to do this work.

## Sorting ideas

There are a few terms which I feel we would do well to sort out in our minds, namely, *activity, pastoral activity,* and *pastoral process.*

The term *activity* hardly requires an explanation. If I run a football team, there is nothing specifically pastoral in itself about that. An agnostic might do the job more effectively. It does have a pastoral potential, of course, Don Bosco, for example, used games to attract teenagers so that he could tell them about Christ.

*Pastoral activity* could be the once-off spiritual event, a retreat, for instance, that has no particular context: no special build-up or follow-up. This is not the best way to go about retreats, but it can happen.

*Pastoral process* could be defined as *a continuous, progressive journey of faith towards clear objectives.* This bears thinking about.

This definition necessarily involves a variety of elements that will require attention within the youth group. They are as follows:

—building community spirit
—appreciating and accepting the person
—promoting Christian commitment
—identifying objectives
—planning and evaluating
—keeping in touch with reality
—shouldering responsibility.

Without wishing in the slightest to question the worth of formative activity or pastoral activity, I believe it is best if there is process at work in the youth apostolate. Where it is present, there is much more likelihood of young apostles such as Vatican II envisaged emerging.

## The Ripple Effect

The ripple effect that we noted emanating from the small Christian community may also be observed on the youth scene. You will find that, when a core community of dedicated young Christians is formed, other young people tend to swirl about it.

Within the first circle we of course find the core group; within the next a considerably more numerous band of young folk, connected with the core group in some special way, usually through a shared apostolate; and, finally, beyond these there is the great amorphous mass of youth towards whom the influence of those within the first circle and their helpers in the second ripples out. Diagramatically, the position can be expressed:

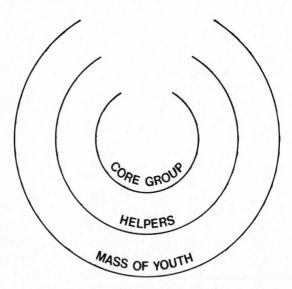

## Respecting Process

Youth groups do need the help of adult assessment for the simple reason that the members are growing in maturity while the adult is presumably mature. At times it is necessary for example to make young persons reflect so that their immaturity does not betray them into foolhardy action. It is not a question of agreeing with their every whim.

The adult assessor, however, be that person priest, religious, or lay, must *respect the process* of the group. He must allow the young people gradually to assume responsibility in accordance with their growing capability until such time as, with adult backing, they are in command. For the adult assessor to monopolise control would be to keep the group in a state of childish dependency. Where there is respect for process, there is a much greater chance of continuity. Where it is lacking, there is the increased risk that with the departure of the adult assessor the community will collapse.

## Overall Christian Youth Movement

Sometimes in a country one finds many excellent Christian youth groups where process exists. They are, however, unaware of one another's existence, so a sustaining sense of solidarity is lost. I often wondered if this might not be overcome by the promotion of an over-all Christian youth movement which would loosely link subsidiary movements and unattached groups. Such a movement would only include groupings where process is at work. There is no point in enlisting a group which is here today and gone tomorrow.

*A national secretariate* of young folk from varying organisations could then be chosen by the youth themselves — and this is important — with a view to fostering this loose unity among groups and movements. This could be achieved by such means as publications, meetings, rallies, and common projects. The sharing of some pastoral priorities could also promote cohesion. Such priorities could be pursuing peace with justice, fostering youth groups, or being critical of the mass media. Co-existing with the loose unity, there would be a complete respect for the *autonomy* of each movement and unattached group.

Briefly then the format of such a movement would be:

---

**OVERALL CHRISTIAN YOUTH MOVEMENT**

|

**NATIONAL SECRETARIAT**
(to foster loose unity
and common pastoral priorities)

|

**SUBSIDIARY
CHRISTIAN MOVEMENTS AND GROUPS**
(where there is process)

---

*Representation on Church Bodies*

It is important too that young people be represented on Church bodies at all points.

## A Passing Phase

Youth is a passing phase. What the Church must do is not to monopolise the phase, but to *serve* the needs of those who must find their own way through it. The needs may change considerably from one epoch to the next.

## To Think or Not to Think?

Perhaps the greatest service we can render the rising generations is to help them *to think* for themselves when there is so much that conspires against their doing so. Pope Paul VI once remarked that the greatest sickness of our time is that people do not think.

The secret then is to get youth to reflect. Not a matter of pouring information into them. The information thus imparted may well go undigested and unassimilated. By giving out ideas and information, we may momentarily assuage a mental hunger. But when we assist people to think for themselves, we solve their problem for good. It is the mental equivalent of teaching a starving person the use of a fishing rod rather than giving him a fish.

Should we succeed in getting youth to think, there is no telling where it could lead. It is like handing them a golden string. In the words of Blake:

I give you the end of a golden string;
Only wind it into a ball,
It will lead you in at Heaven's gate,
Built in Jerusalem's wall.  *(Jerusalem).*

## Democratising Youth Groups

I have often noticed a tendency for Christian youth movements, groups, and functions to become the preserve of the rather better off. The sons and daughters of ordinary workers are notably absent. This I regard as a serious weakness. Their presence would guarantee a dimension of realism without which the youth apostolate can become hopelessly distanced from life and history.

In São Paulo, Brazil, I found a youth apostolate that was deeply rooted among the poor. Indeed the coordinator for the archdiocese was himself a young workingman.

## The Adult Animator

All that was said about leadership and coordination of the small Christian community applies equally to the adult animator of the youth group. One might add that generous dollops of patience and humility and a keen sense of humour are also most helpful.

I knew one such animator who kept a little ragdoll of a clown on his desk which he looked at when he felt he was taking himself too seriously.

# PART V

## THE CHURCH EMERGING

The small Christian community is the most localised unit of a *community-minded Church*. This much we have seen. It is not indeed that a community model of Church is an established fact. But it is emerging, and the small Christian communities contribute greatly towards its emergence.

Furthermore, the Church emerging emphasises *mission* (service), which is a very strong feature of the small community.

This fresh vision of Church had its ostensible beginning with Vatican II. Yet even before the council the vision was growing silently amid the huts and villages of Latin America. The Spirit who moved in the ample halls of the council and the Spirit who moved in the Brazilian *favela* is one and the same. It is a case of the universal and local aspirations of the Church converging.

# 9

## MODELS OF THE CHURCH

The Church has many facets and can express itself in varying forms. These varying forms in which the Church expresses itself are known as *models* of the Church, and we would do well at this stage to describe these models, if only very briefly. We shall then go on to treat more at length of the two aspects we have already highlighted: communion and mission.

(a) We may look at the Church as a *community;* as people moved by the Spirit to share their entire lives. They do this spiritually (by worshipping together), emotionally (through friendship), intellectually (by sharing ideas), and materially (by being generous with earthly goods). This mystical communion has its origin in the loving and sharing life of the Blessed Trinity.

(b) The Church may be seen as a *herald,* as bearing good news, the Gospel of Jesus Christ.

(c) The Church is *servant.* Following in the footsteps of the Lord who "came not to be served but to serve, and to give his life as a ransom for many" (Matthew 20:28), the Church adopts the same ideal of service.

(d) We can view the Church as a *sacrament,* as a visible sign of something invisible. At baptism we see water poured on the head; this, however, is only the visible sign of a great invisible transformation taking place in the person being baptized. The Church then is a sacrament because it makes the Risen Christ, who is no longer visible in person, visible to the world in the Christian community. The Church is therefore a sacrament of the Risen Lord.

(e) Finally there is the Church as an *institution*. This refers to the structures or organisation: ministry, leadership, grouping, and locale. The organisation of course will be conditioned largely by the model of Church which is being emphasised at a particular time.

# 10

## A COMMUNITY-ORIENTED CHURCH

The Church emerging is *community-oriented,* which means that it is highlighting its community aspect more and more. This is true in document and in life.

A basic theme of Vatican II is, in fact, the Church as communion or People of God. The concern is for *people*.

This merely reflects the sacred scriptures. If indeed we consider the great command of Christ to love one another as he loves us (John 15:12), the two elements vital to it are *communion* and *mission*. To love we must in some ways relate to others (communion) and we cannot relate to others unless there is outreach (mission) of some kind.

The roots of a community-minded Church are, in fact, to be found deep in the New Testament. We find mention of the small community in Acts 2:43-47 and 4:32-37. The Jerusalem Christians met in the Jewish temple and also in other places apart from the temple, so as to assert their unique identity as followers of Christ. Thus in Acts 12:12 we read of their being gathered in the home of John Mark when Peter comes knocking on the door.

And Paul too met with the faithful in various households (cf. Romans 16:5, 11, 14-15).

The Christians at Antioch gathered in small groups and sometimes joined together to form a large assembly. This effort *to relate* groups is noteworthy: it shows a concern for the groups not becoming inward-looking (Acts 14:26-27).

## A New Vision

What is dawning in our times is a new vision of the Church as a *community*. The vision is not absolutely new. The early Christians had it, yet over the centuries it faded considerably. But thanks to a Basil, a Benedict, a Dominic, a Francis, a Clare, an Ignatius, a Teresa, a John Bosco, and other great reformers it was never entirely lost.

The vision begins with the Blessed Trinity. *God is community*. The Father, Son, and Holy Spirit love and share to such an infinite degree that, though *three* persons, they are *one* God.

Then comes humanity, which is a community of brothers and sisters created by God in his own image and likeness (Genesis 1:26-27). Humanity (male and female) is like God insofar as it is a loving and sharing community. But, through sin, this human community was riven within itself and estranged from God.

With time, God (community) was made incarnate in the world in the life of the Jesus of history. This occurred by the power of the Holy Spirit and with the cooperation of Mary. Jesus came as a saviour and mediator to reconcile people to one another and to God. He came, in other words, to restore community (cf. John 14:6).

The Saving Risen Lord, in his turn, does not walk the streets of São Paulo, Nairobi, Melbourne, or Manila as he walked the streets of Nazareth in days of yore. Yet he is made visible in all these places, again through the power of the Spirit, by his Church. The Church is the body of Christ, a communion of communities, and a sign of unity of people with God and people with each other. It perpetuates Christ's work of mediation and re-conciliation.

The Church, however, is a worldwide phenomenon that is becoming increasingly hard to identify even in the parish situation. One of the places where it does become clearly apparent is in the small Christian community.

The Saving Lord, for example, is made present by some small Christian communities that I saw in the Gambia. These groups really animated the liturgy of the wider Christian communities, cleaned up cemeteries, and grew food for the old and the handicapped. All small yet telling signs of the Kingdom.

Establishing the Kingdom of God is the goal of all our striving. We realise, of course, that this will only be fully achieved in heaven, when the human community will be finally reconciled and united in love and so share forever the life of the Trinity.

And so the vision ends where it began — with the Trinity.


## On Its Head

In presenting the above vision we have turned a process on its head. Fundamentally we are talking about a development that proceeds from life experience to God rather than from God to life experience. Above all it is by *living* the life of the Trinity, which is a life of loving and sharing, that we get some inkling as to what God is really like. It is not simply a matter of book knowledge.

Our story should read like this. Just as the *three* persons of the Blessed Trinity are so united that they are *one* God, so should the members of a core group strive to the best of their ability to be so united that, though *many,* they become *one* community.

And that *one community* faithfully mirrors the life of the Trinity and clearly encapsulates the new vision of the Church emerging from Vatican II. In short, the Church must be community because God is community. And it is by living in communion that we reveal God to the world.

# 11

## A MISSIONARY CHURCH

The Church emerging emphasises *mission*. Of its
very nature the Church is missionary (*Decree on the
Church's Missionary Activity,* par. 2).

By mission I do not refer to the traditional
understanding of the word, that is, the sending of
priests, brothers and sisters to alien lands in order to
preach the Good News. The summoning and
sending of such generous, self-sacrificing persons is
of course an indispensable part of missionary
endeavour. Nevertheless it is not the whole story.

I refer above all to the *openness* and *outreach*
towards neighbour that every Christian must have.
Every Christian is a missionary. Every Christian
must live and preach the Gospel, so as to transform
persons and transform the world: in short to
promote the Kingdom of God.

It is a question of bringing the light of the Gospel
to places where it has not reached, and re-enkind-
ling it in places where it once burned brightly yet is
now extinguished. And we are not simply thinking
in terms of geographical place, though that would of
course have to be included. *Place* would also be
areas of life where the writ of the Gospel does not
run: this could happen, for example, in business,
politics, or in the media. We promote Gospel values
in the knowledge that they not only make persons
fully Christian, but also fully human.

If then we give mission an all-embracing under-standing as *outreach,* it will imply a variety of terms: evangelization, prophecy, liberation, and service. Inevitably we shall be focusing on such thinking here. The word *prophecy,* for example, given recent developments in the Church, will require careful consideration.

## Mandla's Story

Of the missionary Church there are beautiful things to relate. I should like to recount one about a young African lad whom we shall call Mandla.

Following Mass in a remote African village one Sunday morning, Mandla approached Fr Victor, a genial, dynamic, Italian priest.

"Fada, I would like to be baptized."

The priest looked at the lad. He seemed very much in earnest.

"Well now, if you want to be baptized, you must show me that you mean business. First of all I want to see you here faithfully every Sunday and then, eventually, we can start preparing you for baptism".

Every Sunday, without fail, Mandla was present at Mass. After quite some time he approached Father Victor once more with his request.

The priest had noted his fidelity and suggested that they go and consult the boy's parents.

"But my parents don't live in this village, Fada. Our home is in Makump."

The priest was amazed. Makump was several hours away on foot along narrow paths between tall elephant grass.

There was a serious snag. Mandla's village was

totally Moslem. The priest explained that, were he to baptize him, Mandla would be the sole Christian in a Moslem community. Without support it would be most difficult for him to persevere in the faith. Under the circumstances the father felt that he could not baptize Mandla.

The lad was utterly crestfallen. Tears stole down his cheeks. Father Victor was moved. Then he had an inspiration. "I'll tell you what," he said to the boy, "if you are truly convinced that Jesus Christ is the Son of God, that he came on earth and died and rose to save us, that he wants us to love and help one another, then you will go back to your village and make him known to others, bring him alive for others. If you gather some people who, like yourself, freely desire baptism, we can give you the sacrament because you will have a support group."

Two years after this encounter I passed through Mandla's village with Father Victor. The youth, by then a personable lad of fourteen, graciously offered me some fruit with both hands after the manner of Africa. In front of his house there was a large wooden cross painted in bold red. And Mandla had twenty adults and eighteen young people preparing for baptism with himself!

This achievement was all the more remarkable if we consider that youth are by no means the vocal element in African society that they are elsewhere. Perhaps the deciding factor was that Mandla not only spoke; he acted as well: helped the young, the old, and the handicapped. In his actions, the message of Jesus came alive.

Equally moving is the story of an old man who lived in yet another African village. He was fast losing his sight owing to river blindness. In former times he had probably been searching the murky bottom of some river for diamonds and had become host to the parasite that causes this affliction. He went to a distant hospital in a vain attempt to stave off the darkness that was engulfing him. Although he was not cured, he did hear about Jesus Christ for the first time, and the Lord touched him. In the loss of sight, he found sight.

A Moslem himself, he went home to his Moslem brother and announced that he was a Christian. The brother banished him from the house.

At his new lodging he beat the rim of a car wheel every morning and evening to summon people. When he sensed that there was a gathering, he would deliver his oft-repeated message: Jesus Christ, the Son of God, was born into this world and died and rose to save us. His great command was that we love one another. This was all he knew. He could say neither the Our Father nor the Hail Mary.

Eventually Anthony, a travelling catechist, heard of the old man's apostolate and went to speak with him. The veteran was overjoyed at meeting another Christian and had an insatiable desire to know more and more about Christ. He and the other people whom he had attracted to Jesus decided that they must have a little church.

The blind old man worked generously at the building site. A child would lead him by the hand as he carried water or adobe blocks.

The effort, however, proved too much for him.

One day he collapsed and was obviously dying.

"Get me the fada, I must be baptized," he pleaded.

The priest was a six-hour journey distant: three hours for the messenger to go, three hours for the father to come.

The old man lay gasping, refusing to die. After what seemed an age, the priest arrived and promptly baptized him. Ten minutes later he was dead.


## Latin American Experience

In Latin America simple *campesinos* (peasants), moved by the Spirit leave their own small Christian communities to encourage others to build similar ones. Usually, before the call, they have been dedicated members of their own groups with experience as coordinators.

When the call does come, they don poncho and hat as protection against the biting cold and bone-chilling mists of the silent high Andes, slip into their sandals, and walk vast distances to evangelize their brothers and sisters. They bring no social prestige with them, no material wealth, and they are not ordained ministers: all they bring is the power of the Word of God within them. This of course is *everything*.

These missionaries create no structures, nor do they organize communities. What they do is to enthuse local people to form their own groups.

While they are absent from home, their family and friends will look after their tiny plots of land, livestock, and meagre possessions. On coming back their minds turn immediately to their next journey.

They are rootless missionaries, belonging to all communities and to none.

It is noteworthy that this initiative came from the Holy Spirit working among ordinary people. There are, for example, forty such missionaries in the diocese of Riobamba, Ecuador: a consolation to its sorely tried bishop.


## A Re-run of Acts

Facts like the foregoing make one feel that we are witnessing a re-run of the Acts of the Apostles in our times.

There is a hymn which says that all over the world the Spirit is moving. We hear little about it on television, radio, or in the newspapers, which seem more taken with bleak news. Nevertheless it is true.

Yes. The Church emerging is indeed outgoing. It is increasingly missionary.

# 12

## THE CHURCH IN THE WORLD

Closely related to the notion of mission is the theme of the Church *in* the world. The Council was emphatic; the Church is not separate from the world; it is meant to be very much a part of the world. The Church does not exist for itself; it is an instrument to further the Kingdom of God.

Where precisely is the Kingdom of God to be found? Wherever one encounters *goodness*, whether within or without the confines of the Church, one finds the Kingdom of God. The Kingdom has also been very aptly described as the graciousness of God breaking through to the world. The role of the Church is to uphold and promote goodness no matter where it exists.

This does not mean that we do not try to attract people to the Church. If we are convinced Christians, we will obviously seek to do so. It is in fact best achieved, not by an introverted Church, but by a Church that reaches out to all humankind.

### Deviations

There are certain deviations of which we must be wary. One is the danger of separating the Church from the world.

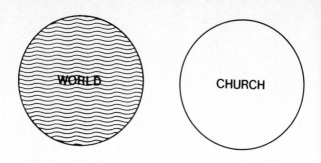

WORLD

CHURCH

This problem is inherent in the existence of the Catholic school and the state school; the Catholic hospital and the government hospital; Catholic press and secular press; Sundays and weekdays. On Sundays we put on our good clothes, go to Mass and communion, and profess love for our fellows. On Mondays we put on our weekday clothes, business becomes business, and heaven help our neighbour!

This can and does lead to a mentality where religion is completely separated from life. Prayer becomes an escape. Mass becomes an escape. And a retreat becomes the great escape.

I am not making a case against Catholic institutions. All I am saying is that in the light of a Church that is meant to be relevant in the world the only justification for the existence of a Catholic school, for example, would be that it open out to all the surrounding community. And it must not simply be a nine-to-five operation.

For me it would also be important that our institutions be not elitest and exclusive. I believe we ought to open our doors to poor people and to such others as find no problem in identifying and sharing with poor people.

Another possible deviation is that we strive to absorb the world into the Church.

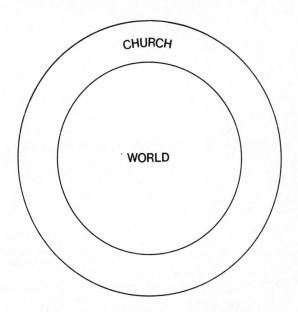

In this scenario all sorts of good but extraneous activities are taken under the umbrella of the Church. A harried pastor may find himself burdened with the boy scouts, dramatic society, sporting club, and debating group. The result is that he may not be able to find time for duties that more concern his priestly office, such as coordinating Christian communities, attending to their integral formation, encouraging apostolic young people, and so on.

Ideally, of course, as the yeast is in the loaf so must the Church be *in* the world.

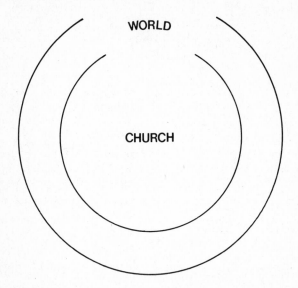

Without the yeast the loaf will not rise. Without a Church that reaches out, the world will not rise.

# 13

## A PROPHETIC CHURCH

One of the most marked ways in which the Church in our times exercises its missionary role is through its *prophetic witness*.

Vatican II speaks of the "prophetic office of the People of God" (*Constitution on the Church,* par. 12), which Christ fulfils not just through the hierarchy but also through the laity (par. 35).

With each passing year, this prophetic dimension becomes increasingly evident as the Church speaks out ever more forcibly on matters of human rights and social justice. One can point to a whole plethora of documents: *Populorum progressio,* (Paul VI, 1967), *Octogesima adveniens* (Paul VI, 1971). *Evangelii nuntiandi* (Paul VI, 1975), and *Laborem exercens* (John Paul II, 1981).

In addition to the popes, CELAM (The Latin American Bishops' Conference) has spoken out at Medellin (1968) and Puebla (1979); and SECAM (Symposium of Episcopal Conferences of Africa and Madagascar) at Yaounde, Cameroons (1981). Following in the path of Medellin, Puebla made a preferential option for the poor.

*Meaning of 'Prophetic'*

The word 'prophetic' refers to those activities

that we associate with the prophets of the Old Testament: announcing justice, denouncing injustice, celebrating justice, condemning idols, and jolting the conscience of leaders, both secular and religious.

When we think of justice, we usually have social justice in mind. The biblical understanding is much richer: it holds that absolutely every aspect of our dealings and relationships with others should be thoroughly moral. It is not simply a matter of economic fairplay. There is, for example, a sad contradiction in the man who struggles for better conditions in his factory and then comes home to ill-treat his wife and children.

In a São Paulo *favela* I heard a woman of African origin say: "I am oppressed three times over; I am oppressed because I am poor, because I am a woman, and because I am black". This set me pondering. After all, the menfolk of her area were most involved in struggling for economic and political justice. Could it be that they were missing even more fundamental aspects? Did they realise that, if they accepted a situation where the women in their midst were unfree, no one was free.

We should obviously try to give justice its full biblical content.

## A Constitutive Part

The 1971 Synod of Bishops declared that *action* (not merely *words*) for justice is a *constitutive* part of preaching the Gospel (*Justice in the World,* par 14). If something is a constitutive part, it simply cannot be omitted. We cannot witness or permit the rich and powerful to exploit the poor and go unchallenged. So the question is not shall we or shall we not do anything about justice; the only question is what exactly shall we do? Given our circumstances, what is the best strategy to adopt? There can be no compromise.

Pope Paul VI says as much when he tells religious, and the same holds for all Christians, that they are not to compromise with any form of social injustice (*Evangelica testificatio,* par. 18). There is no neutrality. To remain neutral is to take the side of the oppressor.

## The Church of the Poor

In recent years the description of the Church as being *of the poor* has become almost a cliché. This description was inspired by the Council and was made still more explicit at Medellin and Puebla.

## Salvation of the Integral Person

The great contribution of Medellin was to make us acutely aware that salvation is of whole persons with their feet solidly upon the ground and not merely of souls considered as vague and floating.

Looked at from this perspective, the one who is hungry, diseased, oppressed, or constantly stalked by immature death does not experience the full liberation that Jesus won so dearly for all of us. This is so, even if that person is free to go to the church and worship.

We need only look at the action of Jesus. He was not content with simply teaching people to pray. He fed the hungry, healed the sick, and spoke out in the strongest possible terms against exploiting widows and orphans. He wanted us to have life and have it abundantly. He evangelized the *whole* person.

## *The Puebla Option*

The great decision of Puebla was *a preferential,* though not exclusive, *option for the poor.* Here again the Church imitates Christ, who placed his pulpit among, and identified with, poor people. From their midst he spoke to the whole of Israel and ultimately to the whole world.

It was not that Christ slammed the door on anyone. When a wealthy person came to him, he invited that person to conversion, to an option for the poor, and to a modest lifestyle. The Rich Young Man sadly declined the invitation (Matthew 19:16-22) while Zaccheus with excessive generosity speedily accepted (Luke 19:1-10).

## *Who are the Poor?*

If the Church is of the poor, then it becomes extremely important to understand who the poor are. Where does one who is educated and cultured (these too are riches) fit into the Church? Where does one fit in who is not lacking in worldly goods?

Puebla has done much fine thinking on the whole question of the poor. It really was a basic theme of the Conference as a glance at the index to the documents will reveal. It gives clear guidelines as to who the poor are.

Firstly the poor are the materially deprived, particularly those unfortunates who are so locked in a struggle for sheer survival, wondering where the next meal will come from, that they are blocked from realising themselves spiritually.

Included too are those who, though having sufficient worldly goods themselves, take up the cause of the poor and are one with them in their struggles. To have enough of the world's bounty is the right of every human being. There is no virtue in misery. Christ came to liberate us from misery. There is virtue, however, in a modest lifestyle: in living simply so that others may simply live. This is part of being a Christian, for we are followers of Christ whose lifestyle was simple in the extreme.

On various occasions I have met people who were at their wits' end as to how best break the apathy of what they called the middle-class Church. But there is no such thing as the middle-class Church. There is only the Church of the poor. So, if a priest were to find himself in a place where people are rather better off, he must urge them to live simply, to share their goods, and to be at one with the disdavantaged at home and abroad in all their strivings.

It is in this way that the well-off are saved. The Puebla option for the poor is not an option against the rich. The conference invites them to liberate themselves by liberating others.

## Approaches to the Problem of Poverty

There are various approaches to the problem of poverty. One is straightforward *aid* to relieve human misery and deprivation. Sadly, it is only too often necessary. When people are starving their immediate need is food, not a discourse on social justice. The difficulty about aid, however, is that, if we give people something for nothing, we somehow lessen them as persons. In aiding people, then, we must strive to preserve their dignity as human beings.

In a certain Third World country the children have a habit of approaching Europeans (whom, not surprisingly, they regard as never-ending sources of wealth) with smiling face, outstretched hand, and the good-humoured request, "Gimme ten pennies". John, a lay missionary, deals with the problem like this. He gives the children machetes, gets them to cut the ever-flourishing grass which threatens to engulf his home, and afterwards gives them some well-earned money. And dignity is thus saved and self-reliance fostered.

Nowadays a youngster approaches and just says, "John, gimme the machete."

Still another approach to the problem of poverty would be to *promote* the deprived through training, education, or whatever. We must try, however, to avoid promoting people who go on to exploit others. Rather should we instil in them a strong sense of service and an appreciation of people above money.

Finally, when dealing with poverty, there is an over-riding need for *structural change* in society, for "bold transformations and innovations that go deep" (Paul VI, *Populorum progressio,* par. 32).

Some folk are poor through circumstances, yet the vast majority of the world's poor are poor because of unjust and oppressive structures. This realisation is facing the Church with an increasingly daunting task: confronting systems of sin. Much persecution has resulted from this stand and the Church is often accused of meddling in politics.

It could be that an individual or an organisation

might be totally engaged in aid such as famine relief, or promotional activities such as schooling; yet, if they do not subscribe to the need for structural change, their vision is quite deficient. With some justification they could be accused of prolonging what is malignant by simply applying superficial lotions, while failing to call for the radical surgery that alone can effect the cure.

## Meddling in Politics

In the current Polish crisis (1982), the Cardinal Archbishop of Cracow, while upholding the rights of workers, was accused by the military regime of meddling in politics. He defended his position and recalled that the same accusation was levelled at Archbishop Romero in El Salvador.

Politics is the active way in which our whole secular life is organised: it concerns itself with health, labour, sport, finance, education, industry and commerce, communications, welfare, or whatever. That is why we have government ministries to look after these areas. Is the Church to have nothing to say in such matters? Must Christians busy themselves with incense and votive candles, or retire to the sacristy? This is precisely what our enemies understand by keeping out of politics. Of course, this is absurd. We cannot opt out of politics, for to opt out of politics is to opt out of life.

## A Balanced View

In the course of my work, I have come into

contact with situations where people have suffered from either an extreme right-wing or an extreme left-wing regime. Both are equally abhorrent. Yet it is not uncommon to find persons with a one-eyed view of the world. Because they suffer, or have suffered, under a right-wing regime, they condemn it vehemently, yet are complacent about the evils of the extreme left. And vice versa. We should not allow ourselves to be used or fooled by either.

Whether someone is standing on your neck with a totalitarian right boot or a totalitarian left boot, the effect is equally excruciating.

The Christian must reach out towards *total freedom* and ultimately settle for nothing less. He will not rest content because his stomach is full if his voice is silenced. He does not have to look to Marx or to Adam Smith for inspiration. Rather does he look to Jesus Christ and measures the worth of all other ideologies against the words of Jesus. He does not live by the Communist Manifesto or the Capitalist Manifesto: he lives by the Nazareth Manifesto:

> The Spirit of the Lord is upon me,
> because he has anointed me to preach
> good news to the poor.
> He has sent me to proclaim release
> to the captives
> and recovering of sight to the blind,
> to set at liberty those who are
> oppressed,
> to proclaim the acceptable year
> of the Lord.
> Luke 4:18-19

What is the relationship between small Christian communities and politics? I believe we can learn from Latin America. The groups that I have known were careful not to allow themselves to be manipulated for political ends. They insisted that the community was *a faith experience.* Of course their experience of faith in the community could motivate them to take a political stand.

In Brazil, for example, they had absolutely no time for the Communists who in recent years have been unmasked as complete, power-seeking opportunists, ready to side with the oppressor to gain a political advantage. I mention this because there is sometimes the idea elsewhere that committed Christians in Latin America are duped by Communists. I have never found it so.

What the communities do exceptionally well is to prepare Christians so that they become acutely aware religiously, socially, and politically. They themselves are then quite capable of freely choosing the parties that most reflect Christian values.

On a chill and clear Andean morning, I heard Francisco, a priest in Ecuador, reflect upon the Word of God as a preparation for the arduous, missionary day he and his companions were facing. Not long before, he had been accused of being a Communist and was in consequence driven from his parish by credulous, simple *campesinos,* instigated by the very ones who were exploiting them, the wealthy landowners. These landowners were enraged by the priest's stand for social justice. During his meditation I heard Francisco insist that the small communities were *faith experiences* and also insist on how wrong it would be to use them for political purposes. Some Communist!

Unfortunately the accusation of being Communist, even if false, is used with lethal effect against good people. I suspect that were he on earth at present, Christ might be labelled a fellow-traveller with the Communists. Especially if he re-issued his Nazareth Manifesto!

You must understand the psychology of privileged people. They are, not surprisingly, committed to the existing order and they see no reason why things should be radically different. Communism for them is very often anything which threatens privilege.

It is interesting to get a glimpse into the dark recesses of this mentality and see the way exploitation is rationalised and justified.

I remember a civilised, cultured, and indeed friendly Latin American lady assure me that the Indians were not like us. They were bad. Ignorant. Inferior.

That was after she saw the horror register on my face as her strikingly beautiful daughter coldly suggested that, when an Indian was guilty of pilfering, he should have a finger lopped off each time he was caught, to teach him a lesson. She did not seem to recall that her forebears had despoiled the hapless Indian of everything he possessed.

To finish the story. In a meeting which followed these remarks, I chose the scripture reading from Matthew 25 ("I was hungry and you gave me to eat, thirsty and you gave me to drink . . .") and talked about love being the only thing that mattered in the end and how there was no question of love where justice was ignored . . . Someone wanted to know what the way she treated the maid in the kitchen had to do with religion. Wasn't religion between her and God? I will always remember the smouldering hostility in the daughter's eyes as she showed me out after the meeting.

We must bear in mind that, though we testify against the godlessness of the Marxist system, it is not Communism itself but the evils which *cause* Communism that are the real enemies of the Church and of humankind. The evils of hunger, disease, oppression, and premature death caused by the insensitivity of human beings to their own kind.

## Need for Prophetic Witness

In our world, thirty million will die of hunger this year. Every minute one million dollars plus are spent on the making of arms. If a moratorium of two weeks were declared on the manufacture of lethal weapons, and the money saved were given to the needy, the basic food and health problems of the planet could be solved for a whole year.

At present 30% of the world's population, dwelling largely in the affluent North, consumes 76% of the planet's substance, which leaves a meagre 24% for the 70% who live in the impoverished South. And the gap grows steadily wider.

Everybody lives now with the menace of nuclear annihilation, and Pope John Paul II recognised this when he said at Coventry, England, on 30 May, 1982:

Today, the scale and horror of modern warfare — whether nuclear or not — makes it totally unacceptable as a means of settling differences between nations. War should belong to the tragic past, to history; it should find no place on humanity's agenda for the future.[6]

Only days later, he went still further when he said in Argentina that all wars are "absurd and always unjust".[7]

It is a moot point whether a way of life that spawns horrendous weapons to preserve itself is worth preserving at all.

Millions of unborn babies are deprived of their most fundamental human right: the right to life.

Persons are discriminated against on the grounds of religion, race, and colour.

Old folk walk the streets of Dublin to keep their feet warm. Old people eke out their lives in isolation from their families in an old person's home in New York. Little ones are discarded by their parents on the streets of many a city.

One day in Latin America I took up a newspaper and read a brief article that created something of a watershed in my own life regarding social justice. It told of a young man who had collapsed and died on the street of acute anemia. Out of work, he had in desperation been selling his blood to the same bloodbank so as to feed his wife and baby. There was a public outcry. The case was referred to the inevitable Presidential Commission, where it no doubt languished and died.

There is sore need for a prophetic Church.

## In the Footsteps of the Master

In being prophetic the Church is merely following in the footsteps of its Founder. The most astoundingly prophetic act in history was when he became flesh and dwelt among us. As Paul says, "though he was rich, yet for your sake he became poor, so that by his poverty you might become rich" (2 Corinthians 8:9). Rich, that is, in the gifts of the Spirit.

# CONCLUSION

I have tried here, largely from life experience, to give an account of the small Christian community with its many ramifications. It has been a human endeavour. Much human effort must also be expended in developing the small Christian community. Nevertheless we must always remember that we are not alone. The work we do is God's work and we are merely instruments.

# NOTES

*Chapter One*

1. *The Tablet,* 9 August, 1980, p. 787.
2. *Newsletter* (Salesian), Dublin, December, 1979, No. 31.
3. *Report: Course on Small Christian Community,* National Pastoral Centre, Kenema, Sierra Leone, 1982, p. 8.
4. cf. *Seeking Gospel Justice in Africa,* Gaba Publications, Kenya, 1981.
5. *Pro Mundi Vita Bulletin,* April 1980, "Basic Christian Communities in the Church", p. 30.

*Chapter Thirteen*

6. *The Tablet,* 5 June, 1982, p. 571.
7. *Newsweek,* 21 June, 1982, p. 27.

# FURTHER READING

*African Cities and Christian Communities,* Gaba Publications, Spearhead n. 72, June 1982.

AMECA: *Afer,* Gaba Publications, P.O. Box 908, Eldoret, Kenya. (cf. vol. VII, no. 4: vol. XV; vol. XVIII, no. 3; vol. XIX nos. 2-6; vol. XXI, no. 5). These articles provide a wealth of theological reflection and practical pastoral suggestions regarding small Christian communities. They are of special interest for Africa, but would be thought-provoking for people anywhere.

Barreiro, Alvaro, S.J., *Basic Ecclesial Communities — The Evangelization of the Poor,* Orbis Books, Maryknoll, New York, 1982. This book manifests a firsthand knowledge of the small Christian communities and is solidly based, theologically and scripturally.

Biagi, Bob, *A Manual for Helping Groups to Work More Effectively.* Citizen Involvement Training Programme, Division of Continuing Education, University of Massachusetts, Amherst MASS 01003. A book which reads easily and contains exercises which may be used or adapted for use by small Christian communities.

Bishops' Committee of the Confraternity of Christian Doctrine, *New American Bible,* Nelson, New York, 1971.

Bowe, Paul, O.P., *The Brandt Report: Commentary and Summary,* Dominican Publications, Dublin, 1981. The Brandt Report shows, and Father Bowe underlines the fact, that aside from any considerations of justice mere self-interest should urge the affluent nations of the earth to solve the Third-World problem.

Camara, Helder, *The Desert is Fertile,* Sheed and Ward, London, 1974, and Orbis Books, Maryknoll, New York, 1974. An inspired little volume which has awakened many a person to the problem of the haves and have-nots in the world. Equally it shows the tremendous power for good of small believing groups (Abrahamic communities).

Clark, David B., *Basic Communities — towards an Alternative Society,* S.P.C.K., London. The most comprehensive account of the basic community movement in Britain. David Clark believes that these small communities have implications both for the Church and the world that are far greater than their size would suggest.

Clark, Stephen B., *Building Christian Communities,* Ave Maria Press, Notre Dame, Indiana 46556. The author proposes a comprehensive strategy for re-centreing Christ in the Church, and building up his body in the world by means of Christian communities.

Comblin, José, *The Meaning of Mission,* Orbis Books, Maryknoll, New York, 1977. Father Comblin shows that 'foreign missions' do not exist as places but as areas of human life where God and Gospel values are shut out.

Cullinan, Thomas, *Mine and Thine, Ours and Theirs, an Anthology on Ownership in the Christian Tradition,* CTS, London, 1981. Useful as a resource book.

*Eucharist and Politics* (CIIR and CAFOD).

Dearling, Alan, and Armstrong, Howard, *The Youth Games Book,* I. T. Resource Centre,

Quarrier's Homes, Bridge of Weir, Renfrewshire PA11 3SA, 1980. Useful for exercises.

de Broucker, José, *Dom Helder Camara — The Conversions of a Bishop,* Collins, London, 1979. In an age when the prophetic Church is coming into its own, this book gives us insights into the life and thinking of a man who is one of our greatest living prophets.

*Doctrine and Life,* Dominican Publications, Dublin, (cf. "The New Communities", Rosemary Haughton, May 1977; "Basic Christian Communities", AMECEA, October, 1979; "Village Christianity", Aylward Shorter, October, 1979). These are informative and thought-provoking articles on the subject of Christian community.

Donovan, Vincent, C.S.Sp., *Christianity Rediscovered,* Orbis Books, New York, 1982. I found this book *exciting.* The word may be misleading, but it expresses what I felt. It really forces you to re-think what the Church and mission are all about. It did for me what only a handful of other books have done: it gave meaning to my groping pastoral endeavours, provided me with a new vision.

Dulles, Avery, S.J., *Models of the Church,* Gill and Macmillan, Dublin, 1976. Until I am clear as to what model of Church I operate from, I am bound to be pastorally disorientated. This book helps us to make an option.

Freire, Paulo, *Pedagogy of the Oppressed,* Penguin, Middlesex, England, 1972; and Herder and Herder, New York, 1970. Surely one of the most influential books of our time. The thinking of Paulo Freire has affected many disciplines, including that of theology. Pastoral practice too has been greatly helped by his ideas.

Gutierrez, Gustavo, *Theology of Liberation*, SCM, London, 1974; Orbis Books, Maryknoll, New York, 1973. Gustavo Gutierrez is certainly a beneficiary of Freire's thinking. His theology of liberation is not simply a new branch of theology, but a whole new way of doing theology. It is more a theology of the trenches than of the halls of academe; a theology written in the shadow of the immense poverty and premature deaths of countless millions.

Harrington, Wilfrid, O.P., *Key to the Bible* (3 vols.). Society of St Paul, Athlone, Ireland; Alba House, New York, 1974. These popular volumes help to open up the treasures of Scripture for the reader.

Healy, Joseph G., M.M., *A Fifth Gospel — The Experience of Black Christian Values,* Orbis Books, Maryknoll, New York, 1981. Rev. Joseph Kalem'Imana, Rulenge Diocese, Tanzania, aptly says of this work: *"A Fifth Gospel* is the most timely and most representative work that we can look to on the life of small Christian communities in Africa."

Healy, Sean, S.M.A., and Reynolds, Brigid, *Social Analysis in the Light of the Gospel,* Folens and Co. Ltd., Dublin, 1983. A useful work, which emerged from a series of workshops.

Hirmer, Oswald, *Marx, Money, Christ,* Mambo Press, Gwelo, Zimbabwe, 1981. We must know the various ideologies that claim to have the best solutions to the problems of the earth. To do this we must objectively analyse these ideologies and then decide which one is most in keeping with our Christian principles and opt for that. Unless we do so, we will be quite at sea in our world. We need a model of society as we need a model of Church. To achieve this we will have to struggle, because the media will not help us: quite the reverse. Fr Hirmer's book, however, will most certainly help us.

—— *How to Start Neighbourhood Gospel Groups,* Lumko Institute, P.O. Box 11, 5410 Lady Frere, South Africa. A kit with posters and textbook for learning a method of gospel-sharing.

Holland, Joe, and Henriot, Peter, S.J., *Social Analysis: Linking Faith and Justice,* Centre of Concern, 3700 13th Street, N.E., Washington D.C. 20017. The authors are both very experienced. Recommended.

John Paul II, *Laborem exercens,* CTS, London, 1981.

Kirby, Peadar, *Lessons in Liberation,* Dominican Publications, Dublin, 1981. With the skill of the competent journalist, but a journalist who has a considerable background in theology, Peadar Kirby makes us live the liberation process of Latin America. There is a most enlightening chapter on basic ecclesial communities.

*Keogh, Dermot, Romero, El Salvador's Martyr.* Dominican Publications, Dublin, 1981. As I went through this eminently readable book, I felt that Dermot Keogh had superbly depicted in microcosm that tragedy which is the tragedy of all Latin America.

Lernoux, Penny, *Cry of the People,* Penguin, Middlesex, England, and New York, 1981; Doubleday, New York, 1980. An excellent resource book on the National Security State and on the role of the multi-nationals.

Lobinger, F., *Building Small Christian Communities*, Lumko Institute, P.O. Box 11, 5410 Lady Frere, South Africa, 1981. A kit with large posters and textbook for starting small Christian communities.

McCarthy, Flor, S.D.B., *Let The Light Shine*, Kairos Publications, Maynooth, Ireland, 1982. Father McCarthy has spent many years trying to make the Gospel accessible and intelligible to working-class youth in a Dublin school. This endeavour is the fruit of that experience. When working with groups, I find it a most useful resource book.

McCreary, A., *Corrymeela — the Search for Peace*, Belfast, 1975. The account of a courageous community which is striving to build bridges across the great divides of strife-torn Northern Ireland.

*Medellin Documents*, translated by the United States Catholic Conference, 1312 Massachusetts Avenue N.W. Washington D.C. 20005.

National Secretariate and Hispanic Teams, *Basic Ecclesial Communities*, Ligouri, Missouri 63057, 1980. I found this volume really helpful. It is above all theologically rich, but also practical. It is not a difficult book.

—— *Guidelines for Establishing Basic Christian Communities in the United States*, do., 1981.

O'Donnell, Desmond, O.M.I., *Growing in Love Together*, Dominican Publications, Dublin, 1980. A five-step do-it-yourself programme for groups. It is designed to foster community. Very successful in Australia.

Paul VI, *Populorum progressio*, CTS, London, 1967;

—— *Octogesima adveniens,* London, Catholic Institute for International Affairs, 1981;

—— *Evangelii nuntiandi* (with commentary by Bede McGregor O.P.), Dominican Publications, Dublin, 1977.

*Puebla and Beyond* (ed. John Eagleson and Philip Scharper), Orbis Books, Maryknoll, New York, 1979.

*Pro Mundi Vita Bulletin,* "Small Christian Communities in the Church", April, 1980, p. 30. The small Christian community has come to be so identified with Latin America that we can easily forget it is a worldwide phenomenon. This article helps to put the communities in their true universal perspective.

Reichert, Richard, *Simulation Games — for Religious Education,* Saint Mary's Press, Christian Brothers Publications, Winona, Minnesota, 1975. This has been found to be a useful source of exercises for groups.

Research and Development Division, National Council of Young Men's Christian Associations, 291, Broadway, New York, N.Y. 10007, *Training Volunteer Leaders — A handbook to train volunteers and other leaders of programme groups.* This work also has helpful group exercises.

Rodger, Charles, S.J., and Maclaren, Drostan, O.P., *The Social Teaching of Vatican II,* Plater Publications, Oxford; and Ignatius Press, San Francisco, 1982. A useful resource book, but sizeable and daunting for the average community member.

Sacred Congregation for Religious and Secular Institutes, *Religious and Human Advancement,* 1981.

SECAM, *Seeking Gospel Justice in Africa,* Gaba Publications, Eldoret, Kenya, 1981.

S.H.E.R.C. Publications, *Handbook of Social and Health Education,* Cork, Ireland. Another source of helpful exercises.

Simon, Sidney B., *Meeting Yourself Halfway,* Argus Communications, Niles, Illinois 60648, 1974. Still more exercises.

*The Jerusalam Bible,* Darton, Longman and Todd, London; and Doubleday, New York, 1966 (complete edition).

Torres, Sergio, and Eagleson, John, Editors, *The Challenge of the Basic Christian Communities,* Orbis Books, Maryknoll, New York, 1981. Reflections on basic Christian community by some of the most eminent people in the fields of theology and pastoral practice from the Third World.

Vanier, Jean, *Community and Growth,* Darton, Longman, and Todd, London, 1979. A veritable gold-mine of reflective and practical ideas on Christian community.

Vatican II, *Conciliar and Post-Conciliar Documents* (ed. Austin Flannery O.P.), Dominican Publications, Dublin, 1975; and Costello Publishing, New York, 1975.

—— *More Post Conciliar Documents,* do., 1982.

White, Mary B., and Quigley, Robert N., *How the Other Third Lives — Third World Stories, Poems, Songs, Prayers, and Essays from Asia, Africa, and Latin America,* Orbis Books, New York, 1977. Useful source material for meetings.

# KEY PUBLICATIONS IN OTHER LANGUAGES

*French*
Lapointe, Eugene, *Des commautēs chretiennes enracinées et responsables. Expērience du Lesotho,* Universitē de Montrēal, Mars 1981.

*Portuguese*
Betto, Frei, O.P., *O Que e Comunidade Eclesial de Base,* Editore Brasiliense, São Paulo, 1981. This is one of the very best little productions on the subject of small Christian community. It is especially relevant to the Brazilian scene, but can be universally helpful.

────── *O Fermento Na Massa,* Petropolis, Editora Vozes Ltda, Brasil, 1981. This is an account of a gathering whose historical significance may not have registered as yet. It was an assembly of lay representatives from Brazilian small Christian communities gathered together at Itaici (1981) for evaluation and reflection. Pastors were also present, but largely in a listening capacity. They wanted to hear the Holy Spirit speaking through their people. I do not know of any meeting comparable to this in the modern Church. Someone even made bold to call it the layman's Vatican II.

*Spanish*
Marins, José y Equipo, *Comunidad Eclesial de Base, Focos de Evangelización y Liberación,* Colegio Don Bosco, Quito, Ecuador, 1981. As stated in our Introduction, Father Marins has

promoted small Christian communities up and down the Americas and elsewhere in the world for more than a decade. He is a man of immense experience. This is his basic book.

Proaño, Loenidas E., *Conscientización, Evangelización, Política,* Pedal, Salamanca, 1974. Of this book I can say what I said of Fr Donovan's above: "It did for me what only a handful of other books have done: it gave meaning to my groping pastoral endeavours, provided me with a new vision". Bishop Proaño's long pastoral experience is evident on every page.

—— *Asambleas Cristianas,* Ed. Paulinas, Bogotá, Columbia, 1975. In this volume we find guidance for a series of meetings to prepare the ground for small Christian communities.


## Recent Publications

Byrne, Tony, CSSp., *Integral Development — Development of the Whole Person,* Mission Press, Ndola, Zambia, 1983.

Dorr, Donal, *Option for the Poor: A Hundred Years of Vatican Social Teaching,* Gill and Macmillan, Dublin; Orbis Books, New York, 1983.